go
where your
EYES
take you

To Our Survivors,

We are eternally grateful to you for sharing your stories of hope, faith, and determination. You have educated and inspired our children so that your memories of the past will not be forgotten in the future. Your acts of heroism, self-sacrifice, and courage will be etched in our hearts and minds forever.

The Spielman Family
Gail, Effie, Jennifer and Jeremy

The Koffler Family
Marcie, Barry, Zak, Micah and Caleb

acknowledgments

The *Shachar Project* is a multi-faceted, year long educational unit designed to study and celebrate the stories of 23 survivors of the Holocaust and the rebuilding of their lives. Our goal was to have our students meet, listen and learn how these men and women were able to survive and start anew. Their stories were to be collected and written so that we learn of the richness and value of living and so that we ensure that their experiences will never be forgotten. From the moment we began, Shachar took on a life of its own. Our Atlanta community embraced it, and we found more and more survivors willing to participate. Faculty, parents, students and community members all contributed to the compilation of this book. What is more amazing is that we were able to complete the book and simultaneously carry on with our normal school program.

I am indebted to English teachers Terri Jacobson and Holly Chesser who attended the interviews and soon became caught up with each survivor. Riveted by the stories, Terri and Holly worked tirelessly with the student interviewers and writers; researching, writing, editing and revising became daily chores interspersed with and following their daily classroom duties. I recognize that the hours spent and work done equals another full time job. My sincerest thanks also go to Dan Berger, parent volunteer, who made himself available to work with individual writers and edit endlessly. He taught us how to "get it right" by checking all details, places and dates.

acknowledgements and thanks also go to:
Jane Cohen and Sandi Morgan, South Area Solomon Schechter School of Massachusetts for sharing their L'Chaim curriculum and starting the idea.

Stan Beiner, Head of School, for entrusting this project to me.

Jane Robbins, Hedva Weiner, and Heidi Cohen, chairwomen of the *Shachar Project*.

Sara Ghitis for her sensitivity in teaching us how to conduct oral interviews.

Monica Rawicz for design of the Shachar logo.

Ety Nes-Ya for her Hebrew translations and creativity.

Fred Katz, who photographed each survivor.

The writers, interviewers, and archivists who had the talent and motivation to do the job.

Jane Levy and Sandy Berman of the William Breman Jewish Heritage Museum for opening the archives to us.

Michele Brown for editing completed student work.

Madeline Rothbard for coordinating the Virtual Museum.

Matt Blum, Jan Lewin and Leora Wollner for coordinating the archive collection of memorabilia and photos.

Lori Miller for organizing the portrait sittings.

Joan Stuart and Lisa Frank for fund raising and publicity.

Judye Groner, Zack Marell and Sue Corns of Lerner Publishing Group.

Gene Rubel for his Hebrew proficiency and never-ending encouragement.

And finally, Heidi Cohen, who kept us on track and on schedule by managing the myriad of lists and assignments associated with publishing a book.

And of course, our thanks and appreciation go to the survivors for both trusting us with their stories and for participating in our school programs.

Myrna Rubel
Middle School Principal
The Epstein School
March 2004

foreward

The meaning of Shachar—dawn—is especially appropriate as these stories of renewal were written by youth, teenagers of The Epstein School. We as English teachers contemplated what participation would mean for our students when presented with the proposal for this Holocaust project. They would learn how to conduct oral histories, compose individual stories, and determine which photographs best captured the survivors' ordeals.
What we didn't take into account was what would become the most important outcome of this project – our students would establish real connections with these men and women.

Every Holocaust story resonates with the need for remembrance. History has taught us that the retelling of each individual story helps us not only to honor these memories, but also to embrace the lessons inherent in each experience. These stories are not simply oral histories; they are permanent tributes to survivors' perseverance, courage, and will.

As instructors in the classroom, we constantly grapple with ways to help our students personally connect to the literature we teach. The drama of Holocaust literature has always attracted adolescents, but having students make meaning of these tragic experiences that happened many years ago in countries whose names they cannot pronounce provides a challenge. This project, however, was different. Students had many opportunities to interact personally with the survivors which enabled them to ask probing questions. These answers provided insight and built a bridge of understanding between the generations. The necessity for remembrance is kindled in these students who themselves now have a "Holocaust" experience that they can call their own and share with the world.

Holly Reagan Chesser
Terri Senoff Jacobson

table of contents

go where your eyes take you

Emaciated and feverish, Helen knelt before the crucifix, made the sign of the cross, and began to recite the Lord's Prayer, hoping her reverence would appear natural and convincing. The Polish Catholic family, whose doorstep she had knocked on frantically, answered the door by saying, "How are you alive? The Jews go in the oven." Helen quickly responded by saying she stole a Jew's clothes because she was cold in the woods. In truth, she had run away from the 1945 death march where 1,000 other women were taken.

Without realizing they were rescuing a young Jewish girl from almost certain death, the Polish family gave her a bed to sleep in and food to eat. Posing as a forlorn Christian girl caught up in the ravages of the war, Helen remained in their care for many weeks until the Allies declared victory. Then, without explanation, she left them and returned to her hometown in southwest Poland, eager to see if any of her family had survived the Nazis' persecution. Only one brother, among seven siblings, returned, and the two of them slowly began to rebuild their lives.

Five years before on Yom Kippur in 1940, a year after the Germans had invaded Poland, the Gestapo arrived to take all of the Jews to a ghetto.

Helen's father had already died because the Nazis wouldn't let him see a doctor. Helen, along with her family, hid for one week without food or water and could see through the window thousands of other Jews being led away. Finally, one night, Helen's family escaped through a canal of chest-deep water. They split up, and Helen was left with her mother and two sisters. Eighteen-year-old Helen looked out at a potato field and wondered what lay ahead of her. Her mother, knowing her teenager stood the best chance of surviving alone, gave her a gold piece and offered the last words Helen ever heard her say, "Go where your eyes take you." Those words helped her focus on her future, fortifying her strength and faith.

Helen came upon her nephew, a 13-year-old boy, and the two of them simply wandered without direction, but the Germans caught them and sent them by train to Blechhammer, a sub-camp of Auschwitz. Once off the train, the Jews were separated by an SS officer who nonchalantly pointed to the right or to the left. Helen saw the boy being sorted into a line with the old and the weak, which meant certain death. She convinced a German soldier to assign him to labor, but she still never saw her nephew again. From Blechhammer, Helen was sent to Grunberg, a women's work camp in Poland where she had the horrible work of sorting through the clothes of the dead looking for hidden jewelry, diamonds or gold. She also made parachutes for the German soldiers. She was told that if she made even one mistake, she would be killed.

Having witnessed the horrors of Blechhammer and the despair in a women's work camp, Helen does not remember exactly what nourished her will to live during her years in the camp. When she came back to her hometown and found one brother who was still alive, she asked him, "What do I do now? What is my life?"

After liberation, Helen, her brother, and his friend, Moshe, who had lost his entire family, shared a two-room flat in Czestochowa, Poland near the small rural towns where they were born. In 1945, Moshe asked Helen to marry. Although both Moshe and Helen had suffered terribly for being Jews, they did not renounce their faith. Indeed, they clung to their traditions as strongly as before. Helen attended the mikvah before her wedding, where she received the ritual cleansing of her body. With no dress or ring, she married Moshe with the required 10 people, a minyan, in attendance.

Helen and Moshe moved to Germany after their marriage where they lived for seven years. Her husband, along with two friends, Sam and Jack Pila, operated a meat company. Jack moved to Minnesota to learn the dairy business, and Helen and Moshe followed in 1952. Arriving in America, Helen was overwhelmed by the new language and customs. By then, she had had her first son, Sam, and was pregnant with her second son, Jack. She spoke Polish, German, and Yiddish, but no English whatsoever. They were not rich; they couldn't read, and they had no friends. Grocery shopping was particularly challenging. She often randomly grabbed cans off the shelves and placed them in her cart, only to throw them out later when she discovered their contents.

They invested in a dairy farm in a small town near Rochester, Minnesota, building it with sweat labor. By then, Helen and Moshe had three children as their daughter RoseAnn had been born. In 1962, ten years after they had arrived in America, they purchased their first home.

Eventually they invested in a second dairy farm in rural Florida where they moved, and there they had 600 cows. There were few Jews in Minnesota, and even fewer in Brooksville, Florida. In fact, most of their dairy farm customers were rural Southerners who knew nothing of Judaism. Nevertheless, when Helen and Moshe grew their own grain to sell as their house brand, they named it "Zayer Git," which in Yiddish means "very good." The family chuckled to hear customers request their popular feed in a slow Southern drawl.

Helen lives near both of her sons in Tampa. She has raised three

children and has six grandchildren. She recalls her constant prayers to God during the war and her question, "God, where are you?" She still wonders why God allowed so many Jews to die while she survived. Before emigrating from Germany, Helen insisted on visiting the Polish family who had harbored her near the end of the war. She wanted to tell them that two things had saved her life: God and them. However, the family's father refused to accept that she was a Jew, insisting strongly that she was, instead, a Polish Gentile. She, however, refuses to allow expressions of such prejudice to dampen her spirit. Instead, she remains faithful and dedicated to God. She proclaims, "He didn't let me die, so I belong to Him."

breaking the silence

Murray Lynn was silent for years about what he saw and experienced during the Holocaust. But the world's silence was one of the things that caused the Holocaust. Now, he makes it his life's work to speak out about it.

When Murray Lynn, born Moishe Leicht, was 12, the Hungarian secret police forcefully knocked on his family's door in the middle of the night and demanded that they open it. They insisted that Murray's father, a charitable leader in the Jewish community, come with them, but they wouldn't tell the family where they were taking him. He sadly remembers, "Later we found out that he and 20 other Jewish leaders were mercilessly executed in the mountains. Mom was a widow at 36 years old." After the Hungarian police murdered his father in 1942, the rest of the family struggled to stay alive. Murray's mother, a former model and beauty queen, closed down the family clothing store. They had to get by on what food they could raise on their farm. The family had no idea how they would survive without their patriarch.

Before his father's murder, Murray lived with his family in Bilke in eastern Hungary. The Leichts owned a store, lived comfortably, and

had their own farm as well. His father Abraham was active at synagogue and in the Jewish community. There wasn't much tension between Christians and Jews then, less than in other areas. There had been no pogroms, but the children were ridiculed at school as "Christ-killers" and "infidels." "We were taunted as people who were in league with the devil," Murray explains. Despite the ingrained hostility towards Jews that led to Murray's father's death, the Hungarian government, directed by Admiral Horthy, resisted deporting the Jews to Hitler's concentration camps. But in 1944, afraid Hungary might make a separate peace with the Allies, Germany invaded and soon started deporting its Jews.

A month after the Germans took over in March of 1944, the Jews of Bilke were rounded up and sent by freight trains to a ghetto where they stayed for two weeks. From there, they were taken by boxcar to Auschwitz. "My little 8-year-old brother had a blanket tied to his back with some of his belongings. It was a poignant scene and could have been an intensely haunting backdrop for a horror movie," Murray says. When they were being loaded onto trains headed for Auschwitz, the neighbors yelled that they should never come back. Murray's mother, dismayed, said she'd never known their neighbors to be so anti-Semitic. "This experience shook us to the core. Being uprooted from our homes was a devastating and unbearable experience. We knew we were destined to die. We just didn't know how," explains Murray sadly.

When the Leicht family arrived at Auschwitz, there were Sonderkommandos helping unpack the train. The Sonderkommandos were, Murray explains, "Jewish prisoners who worked in the gas chambers and crematoriums. They were the workers who unloaded those trains, took our luggage, and helped the SS sort out our possessions. They were sequestered from us, but they were helpful. They had to clean the cars [and] disinfect them – there were no sanitation facilities." The Sonderkommandos told Murray to lie to the Nazis and tell them that he was 16, two years older than he really was. "I was sturdy and athletic. My brothers were too young. My mom, tall and stately with hazel eyes and chestnut hair, thought that she'd protect them by huddling them together. [But] layer by layer, we were stripped of our identity, dignity, personal possessions." The Nazis separated Murray from his mother and siblings immediately, and Murray watched as his family was marched to the gas chambers.

"I was at Auschwitz almost one year. I worked in the underground factories on construction sites, all night or day carrying 50 or 75 pound bags of cement from the railroad cars to the construction sites," Murray remembers. "The consequence of not being able to do this was instant death. It's amazing how much energy we can summon from within when we are threatened." He continues, "Many collapsed or died. Those who couldn't do it were shot."

Murray also survived a two-week death march near the war's end. At that time, he weighed only 65 pounds, was semi-comatose, and doesn't even remember exactly where he was when the Americans liberated him. Murray was taken to a hospital where he stayed for three weeks. He then went back to his native country, "to look for remnants of my shattered past. What I found was our home occupied by hostile strangers and sorrowful memories." After walking two haunting miles from the train station, Murray knocked on the door of the home where he spent his childhood. He did not recognize the man answering the door, but the man knew him. "The stranger opened the door and was flabbergasted to see me. 'I thought you were all dead,' the stranger stammered. 'I'm a ghost,'" Murray responded. Frightened, the man slammed the door, and when he noticed that the ghost did not vanish, he invited Murray in to stay. "They truly believed I was a ghost and finally left my house because they felt haunted. Probably I was more afraid of [this Nazi collaborator] than he was of me. I knew at any minute I might be killed, and no one would know, and no one would care."

Murray soon realized that he was his family's sole survivor and that there was no future for him in Hungary. Fortunately, he found an uncle living 50 miles from Bilke who had miraculously survived the war too. Murray lived with him for six months. The area, now part of the Ukraine, was becoming increasingly Communist. Murray, afraid of the "Iron Curtain" descending across the continent, then headed west to a kibbutz-style collective farm for Jews in Hungary, where he stayed another six months.

Following his kibbutz experience, Murray decided to go to the Czechoslovakia where it would be easier to get a visa to America. He wanted the peace, freedom, and economic opportunity that America offered. Finally, he made his way to Czechoslovakia, where he applied to a famous yeshiva, the Presburg Yeshiva. "I was accepted there, and it gave me a chance to decide what I wanted to do and take stock of myself," Murray reflects.

About a year later, a British philanthropist, Rabbi Solomon Schonfeld, brought Murray and more than a hundred other Holocaust orphans to Ireland, where they lived in a castle near Dublin. They only had temporary visas for Ireland, but the next year Murray luckily

received a scholarship to study at Yeshiva University in New York, and he came to the United States in 1948.

"When we came to New York it was a tremendous transition for us. We came with hate and prejudice foisted in our hearts. It was a tough adjustment. Layer by layer, we had to peel away fear, degradation, insecurity. It required monumental efforts to purge ourselves of the mindset that kept us powerless." Trying to regain his dignity and faith, Murray was haunted by memories of the war, and this new environment was complicated for him. He also had to regain trust and confidence in people and learn to live in a free economy.

"A healthy self image was critical for rebuilding our lives," he says. "I did this through education. I improved myself by reading, by assimilating, by trying to purge myself of those onerous emotional burdens – the slave mentality." He also decided not to talk much about his wartime experience.

Murray lived in New York for seven years while finishing college and graduate school and studying business and economics. He then moved to Atlanta, Georgia in 1956 where a manufacturing company hired him. Moishe Leicht then Americanized his name to Murray Lynn.

Murray achieved his career and familial goals. He married Sonia Stillman of Nashville, Tennessee, and they had three children. Few of his business colleagues or friends knew about his background because, "I didn't want the past to enslave my future."

The Holocaust shook Murray's religious faith. He considers himself a "recovering Jew." "I felt that our divine covenant was broken by [God] not protecting us. It is something I have struggled with much of my life – to regain my faith in God," he says. Murray Lynn now goes to Temple Beth Tikvah in Atlanta, Georgia, and is

on the board there. "It's a way for me to drift back," he admits.

Finally, he has broken his lifelong silence about his past. Since his retirement, "I began speaking for the benefit of future generations." When asked why he began to open up, Murray replies, "Age had a lot to do with changing my mind. As you get older, you feel you owe this to the community so they can be better prepared to deal in the future with powerlessness and prejudice. Secondly, my friends pushed me into it. They felt I had a terrific story to tell." Murray now speaks at churches, schools, and museums. He wants to get an important message across to today's youth. "Fight bigotry at any cost."

"More than anything else, [young people] must learn to vigorously and zealously protect religious pluralism, one which embraces religious diversity, the cornerstone of a free society. If you encounter racial slurs or bigotry, don't remain silent. The Holocaust," he declares, "happened because too many world leaders remained silent and too few spoke out."

what would·my parents say?

Ruth Scheuer Siegler and her sister Ilse sat in an old farmhouse with a razor blade in their hands. They were two among a handful of survivors of a death march in which hundreds of women had died. Ruth and Ilse contemplated their lives, their future and suicide, a troublesome choice to make when both were gravely ill. Ruth and Ilse had experienced the Holocaust first hand. It was over now, and they had no idea if the rest of their family was still alive. They were exhausted; they were sick, and now they were both on the point of giving up.

Ruth was born in the spring of 1927 in Sinzenich, Germany, where she lived with her parents, Ilse and brother Ernst. Sinzenich was a farming town with only a dozen Jewish families, but everybody respected their neighbors, and Ruth's family was treated the same way as non-Jews. Her family kept kosher, and Ruth went to synagogue and Hebrew school. Her father was a cattle dealer and ran a kosher slaughterhouse. Twenty years later, however, her family's circumstances would change dramatically as they became victims of Hitler's reign.

In 1939, life became unbearable for the Jews of Nazi Germany, so the family left for Holland. They lived there for three years until the

Germans occupied Holland and sent them to the Westerbork concentration camp, where they spent a harrowing two years. The family was sent to Theresienstadt in Czechoslovakia, a "model" camp created by the Germans for inspection by the Red Cross, for a few months and then on to Auschwitz-Birkenau in 1944, where, unknown to Ruth and Ilse, her parents and brother had perished. Ruth and her sister were sent from Auschwitz to the Praust work camp in Poland where they labored building landing strips for airports.

With the war near its end, the Germans wanted to drive the surviving Jews "into the sea" so that their bodies would not be found by the world as evidence of what the Germans had done. They marched Ruth, her sister and hundreds of other women, starving, sick and weak as they were, for a month. They didn't really travel very far, as the Russians were surrounding the area. Eight hundred women started the march, but there were only 50 left alive at the end. Ruth, who now weighed only 80 pounds, and her sister were wracked with typhoid fever. "We were just skin and bone," she painfully recalls.

By the end of the march, only one SS man remained to guard them. Ruth remembers, "He said, 'I'm going. I don't want to be caught by the Russians. You can do what you want.' That's how we were liberated." They walked through some frozen fields, looking for a barn for shelter and knocked on the door of the first farm house they came to. To their wearied dismay, SS troops guarding some French soldiers answered the door. The SS, figuring the two sick and starving girls would die by morning, took no interest in them. The girls went to sleep sitting up on the floor in one of the rooms. "They wanted us to go to bed, but we said no. We didn't know what would happen to us," Ruth explains.

When they woke the next morning, they were alone. The soldiers, the French prisoners and even the farm family had left. Walking to a nearby town, they found a Russian Jewish officer and doctor who spoke Yiddish, a language Ruth had picked up in the camps. He offered to send them with soldiers to Moscow to stay with his wife, but they refused, not wanting to go to Russia. The doctor nursed them for a few days at a large farm house the army had occupied as its local headquarters. While some of the soldiers bothered them, others were nice and cooked for them, although the girls were too sick to eat. Finally, the doctor wrote a document for them, and the soldiers who read it stopped attempting to molest them. The girls still don't know what the paper said, as they couldn't read Russian. Maybe he'd told them how infectiously ill they were, Ruth wondered what was written in the last note.

Soon the doctor told Ruth and Ilse the army had to move on and that they would be left behind. The Polish authorities would find them, he said. "Nobody came for days," she says. "We were in a little room there. We couldn't even get up to get water. We couldn't keep ourselves clean." Desperately ill and possessing a razor blade, the girls contemplated suicide. Yet, they considered the possibility that family members may have survived. "We said maybe we'd find our brother or mother or father. We had hope and that kept us alive. That day, or the next day, they found us," Ruth shares.

Ruth and Ilse were transported to a hospital in Putzig where Ruth had to have an operation. While they were sheltered in a barn during the death march, Ruth was hit by an SS woman with a switch, a glancing blow to the breast that was actually meant for someone else, she recalls. It became infected. She bled so much after the operation that she thought she would die.

In June or July, Ruth and Ilse, measurably stronger and fearful of being sent to a displaced persons' camp, escaped on a coal train to Krakow, and then on to Prague. Although they did not have tickets for the trains, they simply showed the train conductor their tattoos from the camp, and they were allowed on board. The Jewish underground in Prague, helping refugees get to Palestine, gave them clothes and a little money. They told them they had to get out of Prague, which was Russian-occupied, before the Russians sealed off the borders. The girls headed for Pilsen, not far away, where the Dutch army was stationed. The Dutch said they couldn't take them back to Holland without proper documentation and sent the girls to a medical clinic in Bamberg where they received more medical care and, finally, permission to go back to Holland.

They returned to Holland, where they finally learned their immediate family had perished in the death camps. Luckily, they found an uncle and aunt in Utrecht who had survived by hiding in an attic. They took the girls in. "He turned gray when he saw us. They thought we all had died," Ruth recalls. That night, for the first time in years, Ruth slept between clean sheets. They lived with their aunt and uncle until they were able to come to the United States in 1946.

Part of a loving family before the Holocaust, Ruth and Ilse were not used to being in the world alone. Before their father died, he, in preparation for war, had arranged with cousins in Omaha and Brooklyn, New York to sponsor the girls for immigration. Fulfilling their father's wish, in the late 1940s, Ruth and Ilse traveled by boat to the United States without knowing the language or the culture. They arrived on a freighter from Holland to Mobile, Alabama. Ruth loved America from the first time she saw it.

In Brooklyn, finding work and earning money was difficult. The girls' cousin led them around the city to help them look for a job.

Although a glove factory was not Ruth's ideal line of work, she didn't speak English or have a college degree, so she jumped at the opportunity. Night school and movies helped her learn English. Her eyes light up when she recalls memories of watching old movies over and over with her sister in the local theater.

On a holiday to San Francisco, Ruth and Ilse stopped in Omaha, Nebraska to visit cousins. There, she met her future husband, Walter Siegler, whose parents had been friendly with her own in Europe. Fortunately, his parents immigrated to the United States in 1936. Ruth and Walter married and lived in a small midwestern town near St. Joseph, Missouri. They moved to Birmingham, Alabama in 1960 where her husband opened a shoe store. She lost her husband to a heart attack in 1968 and had to raise their three children alone.

While she has only contemplated returning to Germany, she has visited Holland several times. "I've never been back to Germany," she says. Her children have long wanted to go, but she has always felt "I could never go back." However, "they want for me to show them Sinzenich. It's near Cologne, a very small town, in the Rhineland. Now I'm 76 years old, and I want to show them where we used to live." Ruth's children also want to go to Berlin, but she refuses to go.

Ruth still works in the shoe store in Birmingham. She has seven grandchildren and has never been happier. She is active as a volunteer at her synagogue and museum. She loves her job, her family, herself, but most of all, she loves the right to practice her religion freely.

Ruth never told her children about her Holocaust experience until they were adults. Looking back, she finds that the love her parents showed her in childhood gave her strength during her ordeal. "You have to believe in something," she declares. "I kept believing and hoping. I was still a child. That's what kept us going, that maybe we would see our family again." The memory of her parents is still with her. Whenever she makes a decision, she says, she thinks about what her parents might say. Even during the worst of her experience, digging ditches and shivering with disease at Praust as hundreds died around her, she fasted on Yom Kippur and said her prayers at night. Her faith and her parents' love kept her alive.

sam silbiger

from inmate to freedom fighter

Pow! The kids walking to school froze at the sound of the shot. What was going on? Planes flying overhead; a mysterious gunshot had just been fired, and the year was 1939. Among those kids walking to school was Sam Silbiger. He knew something was wrong; his father was always listening to the radio, and his family was scared. Sam would soon learn it was for good reason.

Sam was born in a little Polish town Oswiecim, where his ancestors had lived for 400 years. It's better known today as Auschwitz, what the Germans called it, and most of Sam's family died there in the concentration camp. Both of his parents came from families that owned brick factories, and their bricks had been used for years for construction around town, including Polish army buildings. It's possible, says Sam, that some of the infamous camp's buildings contained bricks made by his family.

Sam's father was a Zionist. Sam was a member of Betar, the conservative Zionist movement, and remembers hearing its famous leader, Zev Jabotinsky, speak in 1935. Sam's father employed Jewish students on his land who were preparing to go to Palestine to work on kibbutzim, collective farms. They needed to learn how to work hard.

"My father paid them well," Sam recalls proudly. His father wanted to go to Israel himself, but Sam's mother became pregnant, and they needed to look after the family's businesses in Oswiecim instead.

When the war intruded into their town, Sam's father became worried as the family lived so close to the Polish army barracks. When the Polish army began fleeing from the German invasion, Sam's family fled too. They escaped by horse and wagon and moved ten kilometers to sleep in their neighbor's barn. The next day, Sam's mother returned to the farm to check on the animals and to determine if it was safe to go back home. She learned that Germany, having defeated the Polish army, now controlled Poland. Indeed, as the family returned to their home, they found bodies of dead Polish soldiers along the river.

Little by little, the German army took Polish citizens' weapons and valued possessions. Sam's father, working as a corporal and a medic in the Polish army, entrusted his gun, wrapped in heavy paper, to 16-year-old Sam who hid it in an unused latrine. Next, the Germans began taking away food and other necessities from the Jews. Soon afterwards, the Germans rounded up the adult male Jews, sending them to work camps to help prepare the Germans for war.

In 1940, Sam's father was sent to work as a slave laborer on the construction of the Autobahn, Germany's highway system. He was released when the Germans discovered that he fought for Germany in World War I. While Sam was sent to a village in the mountains to work for the German soldiers, his family, including his recently released father, was sent to Auschwitz. In 1942, Sam, along with his fellow Jewish workers, was sent back to the Autobahn barracks, but this time to break them down and send them on trucks to a new site. Although Sam was in relatively good health, he was surviving often on spinach, thick with sand and dried potatoes. He remembers seeing the food boxes delivered for use in the camp labeled, "Only for use for Jews, Gypsies, and Pigs."

In 1943, Sam's group moved from working on the construction of the Autobahn to Blechhammer, a sub-camp of Auschwitz, where he united with his father. Sam was quickly reduced from a man with a name to a "dirty Jew" with a tattooed number, striped uniform, and hat. Put to work building barracks, he recalls never receiving a beating, explaining that as a hard worker, he never gave them cause. Czech civilians would sometimes come and work with the Jews side by side, and with extra scraps of food, Sam was able to get by. "There was always something left over, but you always had to make sure not to get caught," he emphasizes. However, he recalls the difficult psychological torture of the camps. One day American planes dropped bombs nearby. Three Jewish prisoners from the camp ran to get wire from the debris to use as belts to hold up their pants. German soldiers hanged them on the spot and left their bodies on display for days. Each morning and night as Sam went to and from work, he and other prisoners had to pass the gruesome sight.

In January 1945, the Russians attacked and 4,000 prisoners were forced on a death march in freezing weather from Blechhammer to Gross-Rosen, a concentration camp in Poland. Anyone who fell was shot to death. Other prisoners from Auschwitz joined them in the march. After a short time at the new camp, they were herded into cattle cars and taken to Buchenwald, another concentration camp in Germany. There were 100 to 150 prisoners crowded in each car, and few survived the journey. Once they arrived at Buchenwald, they were undressed and told they were going to be deloused. Sam, thankful that he was still with his father, knew this was the end. They quietly walked into the shower, soap in hand, and waited; to their relief, water – not gas – poured out. Over the next two weeks, they were only fed twice.

The Germans then took the remaining prisoners on a train to Dachau where they were forced to perform meaningless work simply to keep them occupied. On April 28, 1945, Sam and his father were once again forced on a train and sent to Mittenwald, near the Austrian border. Taken off the train, the Jews were commanded to lie down on the ground so the Germans could machine-gun them. Luckily, an SS commander stopped the soldiers from carrying out this command; Sam suspects the commander's wife convinced him to disobey his orders.

The next morning, the Jews woke up to find the guards gone. Each of the officers had carried a backpack with civilian clothes which they apparently donned, leaving their army garb on the ground. Sam, wearing one of the discarded SS shirts to keep warm, began with his fellow prisoners the slow trek back to town. Weighing less than 70 pounds, he was extremely weak and could barely walk. The German citizens in the village fed the Jewish survivors thick soup with bacon in it. Sam recalls, "They fed us death. We all immediately were struck with dysentery." Later, the Americans sent him to an army camp where he was fed Spam and potatoes. He almost died from this rich food, until some American doctors took over and administered charcoal to the sick.

Finally liberated, Sam never attempted to reunite with his family, hearing of horrible pogroms committed by the Polish citizens against Jews who returned. While in a displaced person's camp, he heard radio reports of Jews fighting for freedom in Palestine. "They need soldiers," he realized and decided to join the Irgun, freedom fighters battling against the British Mandate in Palestine. Irgun agents directed him to travel from Lanzburg to Munich and to the Czech border. He and other Irgun members traveled to Marseilles, where they bought a naval ship, the Altalena, from the Americans. Additionally these refugees bought arms from the French, recognizing that they may have to defend themselves on their journey. With 900 people on board, most of them hidden in the hold so that it would look like a merchant vessel, they sailed to Palestine, ready to fight if the British stopped them. Bravely, they made a run into Netanya and quickly unloaded all the arms. Menachem Begin, later Israel's prime minister, came to welcome them, and the organized Palestinian Jews brought them immediately to Bet Olim, the House of Newcomers.

Sam served in the Irgun for 15 months and then was discharged. Shortly after, he received a letter from his father, recovering in a Frankfurt sanitarium, saying he needed his son's help, and in 1950, Sam was permitted to leave.

In Germany, he took care of his father and worked as a carpenter. In 1955, he married Margot Melzer, a German woman, and in 1956, they came to the United States, joining Sam's sister and her family in Kansas City. Sam worked in a luggage factory, saving enough in two years to buy an apartment building where, he proudly remembers, "I was the owner, the carpenter, the electrician, the roofer – everything from A to Z." In 1961, just after their daughter Eva was born, they followed Sam's sister and her family to Atlanta, and Sam opened a grocery store. However, after ten years and five robberies, he'd finally had enough and closed the store. He went into the real estate business and is now retired. True to a life of being handy, he keeps busy puttering around his property. "I have a big house and a big yard and a swimming pool, and I do everything that is supposed to be done around the house. What I can do, I do it."

Seven years ago, Sam returned to Poland with his daughter and his wife. He took a photo of one of the brick factories, which was in bad shape and possibly going to be torn down. During his visit to his village, he recalls greeting the man who lives in his family's home. The Polish man, with whom Sam was familiar, replied derisively, "You Silbiger? You lived? You Jewish, then how come you lived?" Sam asked the man for some memento from his family who had lived on that land for 400 years, something he could give to his daughter, but the man said he had nothing at all to give.

i guess god fell asleep

Living in a displaced person's camp in Berlin in 1946, in a two-story building with four people to a room may not seem like paradise, but Shoshana Bank remembers feeling "very much protected." She took nightly trips to the theater to see an opera and taught at a Hebrew school during the day. After years of forced hard labor in Russia, Shoshana cherished her liberty. Shoshana proclaims, "We were free!"

Shoshana was born in 1925 in Ponevez, Lithuania, a town with a large Jewish population. Her father owned a general store in Subacius, a small town nearby, and her mother was a housewife. Shoshana had five siblings and was one of the middle children. Although Hitler came to power in the early 1930s, the situation did not become difficult for her family until 1939 when the anti-Semitic movement grew increasingly stronger, worrying Shoshana's father deeply. Shoshana herself was an avid reader, so, reading the paper, she too became aware of the strain. When the Russians occupied Lithuania in 1940, they took over the store, confiscating rooms for their offices. Additionally, the Russians abolished all of the Jewish holidays. Nevertheless, Shoshana remembers the Russians as being polite, "much better than the Nazis." They even allowed her father to continue managing his

store for a while.

Because Shoshana attended a Jewish high school for girls in Ponevez, she saw her parents only on holidays. She lived with a local Jewish family while studying Hebrew, Bible, Jewish law, history, Latin, German, science and math. She learned to speak many languages. During her first year of high school, she missed her family but adjusted to and loved her second year. She explains that it was different from today as the teachers were very strict and stern. The last day of high school was in June 1941. The final exams were on a Saturday, and the next day the war broke out. Germany invaded the Soviet Union and Lithuania as well. That, she says, "was the end of our dreams."

Immediately, she received a telegram from her mother telling her to come home, but Shoshana had no way of getting there. She recalls the pandemonium of that day with people running in every direction. She thought, "Our past will lead us into the future." Following others, she fled with only the clothes on her back to Russia, ultimately into the center of the country. As a refugee, she was sent by the Russians wherever they wanted her. Initially, she worked on a Russian collective farm, called a kolkhoz, in Yoshkarla, 400 kilometers east of Moscow, and later another in Uzbekistan where it was not so cold. She performed hard labor, digging to prepare the ground for cotton.

In the kolkhoz, she saw an announcement asking young people to join trade schools. She signed up and was accepted to a trade school in Tashkent, Uzbekistan. Before the war, she had studied languages, Torah and math. Now she would learn to be an electrician. Following her studies, Shoshana was assigned to a factory in Berezniki, in the Ural

Mountains in Siberia, to work as an electrician's assistant, but she became ill and was released around 1943. Since the war was coming to an end, she traveled to central Russia. There she received a letter stating that her family was dead, killed by the Germans along with the other Jews in town. "I cried for a day and that was it," she says matter-of-factly. "I only thought of moving forward." One sister, Helen, along with her husband, did actually survive by escaping into Russia.

Alone, Shoshana returned to the kolkhoz in Yoshkarla, where she still knew people and stayed until the war was over. The Russians labeled her a "Westerner" and let her leave the country. Aided by a secret Zionist organization, B'recha, set up to help refugees, she traveled to Poland and then Germany. She wound up in a displaced person's camp in the American section of Berlin in 1946 where she was protected. There, she lived in a room with three other people in an old army barracks, ate in a kosher dining hall, and received clothing. The camp was one of a few in a big city which had definite cultural advantages. By day, she taught Hebrew and Yiddish at the camp's school. By night, she could enjoy such entertainment as the camp provided or go into town to see movies, opera or concerts.

During the Russian's blockade, when a wall was built around the city, Shoshana's camp was evacuated, and military planes took the refugees to Munich. Shoshana went to work at the Jewish Agency for Palestine in Munich for two years, where she helped resettle refugees. She says, "I was happy there. I was very, very happy with my job." When,

the Jewish Agency closed in 1950, Shoshana began working for the Jewish Joint Distribution Committee, also known as "the Joint." She worked in the department of education for the Israeli emissary who supervised the DP camp schools.

While in Munich, at a seminar, Shoshana met her future husband Irving. Irving, a Dachau survivor, also worked for the Jewish Agency of Palestine in its economics department and led tours to Israel. They kept in touch through letters and became engaged. In 1951, the Joint sent them to Toledo, Ohio to continue their work. In Ohio, Shoshana and Irving married and moved to Detroit, Michigan to live in a larger Jewish community.

Shoshana and Irving have two daughters, Shelli and Naomi. Shoshana briefly became an after-school Hebrew teacher at the Labor Zionist's School but left to raise her children. She returned as a Hebrew teacher to work for United Hebrew Schools of Detroit, a job she held for 38 years. During these years, she never shared her Holocaust experience with her students because many of her students were themselves survivors or children of survivors, and no one spoke of their tragedy. "My job was to teach them, not to have personal discussions," she says. She explains that talking about the Holocaust has only recently become acceptable.

Shoshana and her husband retired to Atlanta 15 years ago. They have three grandchildren. Her sister Helen lives in Florida.

Throughout Shoshana's experience, she explains, "I never questioned Judaism; it was always a part of me." She struggled with questioning God, and says despondently, "I'm not a theologian. I'm not a psychologist. I guess God fell asleep." Today, she is very optimistic about the future of the Jewish people whom she believes are blessed with a special ability to flourish. Her message to children today is "Keep doing what you're doing. You are privileged. You live in the greatest country in the world, the United States. Be appreciative of the freedoms you enjoy!"

faith, fate and a miracle

Strains of the Avinu Malkenu song from the Day of Atonement liturgy rose softly from the back room. The back room was supposedly a storage area, but today it had other purposes. Tucked away were five occupants, fighting for their lives. Loud voices emanated from the dining room, praising Hitler and his dealings with the Jews. The five Jewish men huddled together, terrified, but proud of their faith. Their cramped hiding spot became a synagogue. A man named Isaac, who had a good voice, became the cantor. It was Rosh Hashanah in 1945, and the five men were conducting Rosh Hashanah services in the closet of a Polish Gentile home. As Isaac put it in his book, By Fate or By Faith, "We were uplifted spiritually to the highest degree that a human can aspire to achieve. The little invisible spark inside us ignited, and that was something not even the Nazis could take from us."

Isaac was a young man, fresh out of a labor camp in Poland. Early one morning, with a few crumbs of matzah in his pocket from a seder years earlier, Isaac and his friend Pinya had jumped over the fence in a daring escape they planned for months. They ran to a nearby farm owned by a Polish family named Marcinkowski. The Marcinkowskis were anxious about hiding Jews, but nevertheless allowed Isaac and

Pinya to hide in their storage closet in the back of the house. Thus began a new chapter in Isaac's life. The old chapters were still painful to remember.

Isaac was born Itche Gutfraind in Piotrokow, Poland in 1924. He was the oldest of five children, three boys and two girls. His family belonged to a devout Jewish sect called the Alexander Hasidim. They were deeply committed to their faith. At the age of 3, Isaac began his formal Hebrew education in a cheder near his home. Within a year, Isaac was able to read Hebrew almost fluently. Thereafter, Isaac began accompanying his father to services. Isaac's father had an excellent voice and expected 4-year-old Isaac to recite the prayers along with him. At 5, Isaac began learning the Bible, and within a few years, started Talmudic studies. In 1937, following his Bar Mitzvah at 13, Isaac was sent to a yeshiva in Sosnowiec. As he grew older, Isaac maintained his unwavering Jewish faith.

By 1941, the situation in Poland was bad for Jews. There were often conflicts between Jews and Germans on the streets. Jews were harassed, beaten, and forced into labor camps. The Germans required all Jews to wear yellow stars on their clothing, but young Isaac cut off his payis, or ear locks, to avoid being recognized as an obvious Jew.

Then disaster struck. Typhoid fever began spreading like a brush fire around Piotrokow. Unsanitary conditions and a lack of doctors added to the flames. Isaac's beloved father contracted the disease and slipped into a coma. The day after Shavuot in 1941, Isaac's father died. Suddenly, 17-year-old Isaac was responsible for his mother and his four younger siblings. At this point, Isaac believed he "grew into a man overnight."

Isaac fell ill with typhoid fever in the early summer of 1942. After quickly recovering, he volunteered to work at a glass blowing factory. The same company had an industrial glass factory nearby. It was a labor camp called Kara. On some days, Isaac worked at the camp if there were not enough workers. One day, the German soldiers assembled the glass blowing workers and read the names of about a hundred people who were sent to other camps, where they later would be killed. Isaac was not one of them. He wonders to this day if he was spared by fate, or instead by his strong faith.

Soon after, Isaac was forced to transfer to Kara permanently. The work there was overwhelming. Isaac compared it to the work Jews did in Egypt during the time of the Exodus. But, he learned to carry his load without complaint, for the consequences were dire. The guards whipped those workers who showed signs of weakness. One day, Isaac received word that he had one hour to go home, pack a knapsack, and gather with other Jewish workers. Quickly retrieving his prayer book and tefillin, Isaac said goodbye to his family, hugged them for the last time, and headed off to a different ghetto. In December 1942, Isaac learned that his mother, brother, and sister had all been murdered in a massacre at the Piotrokow synagogue. One month later, Isaac's remaining brother and sister were seized by the Nazis. Barely 18, Isaac was now alone.

Isaac continued to work at the same factory. His whole world had been destroyed. By fall of 1943, Isaac realized he had to escape the labor camp. With the help of a guard Isaac befriended, and accompanied by his fellow worker, Pinya, Isaac slipped behind a wall and jumped over the fence. It was May 1944. Isaac was free.

Taking refuge now with the Marcinkowskis, Isaac learned how to farm and thresh wheat. The Germans were still rounding up Jews, but Isaac felt safe. The family called him Roman and housed other Jews too. Isaac worked there for nearly a year, diving into a closet when the German soldiers came. One night in January 1945, Isaac was awakened by the sound of the Russians bombing the Germans. Isaac and the other Jewish men, fearing for their lives, sat down and wrote their accounts of these events. They didn't want their stories to be forgotten. Two days later, the Jews were liberated.

Now 21, Isaac returned to Lodz, Poland in search of family on his father's side. There, the Jewish Joint Distribution Committee, known as "the Joint," placed Isaac's name on a register of surviving Jews and gave him an apartment to stay in while he looked for work. Isaac joined Zionist groups as the Lodz Jewish community started to rebuild. One day, a friend from the labor camp asked Isaac to come to Berlin. Unable to find surviving family and still seeking work, Isaac agreed and hopped onto the roof of a train headed to Berlin.

In Berlin, while wandering the streets, Isaac met up with Aharon Saurymper, the landlord of Isaac's relatives in Lodz. Aharon had been in Berlin long enough to establish some connections in the small Jewish community. Aharon was a generous man, and he offered to help Isaac get work and establish himself in the community. Aharon brought Isaac to Friday night services at the home of Jewish chaplain Rabbi Joseph Shubow from Boston. Isaac began attending services regularly and grew close to Rabbi Shubow. Within weeks, Rabbi Shubow, Isaac, and Aharon were establishing the first Joint office in Berlin. Isaac organized challah baking and unearthed a Torah that had been buried in a local Jewish cemetery since the beginning of the war.

In October 1945, Isaac followed the advice of a friend and walked into a restaurant where three Jewish girls were sitting. One of them, Betty Grossman, was 18, attractive, straightforward, and smart. They talked of politics, news, family, and religion. Isaac felt an immediate connection to the young Orthodox Jewish girl, and he was eager to learn more about her.

Betty was born in Vilkija, Lithuania, near Kovno, in 1927. She was the seventh of nine children of Bella and Mordechai Grossman. When she was a baby, her family moved from Vilkija to a city near the German border called Kalipeda. But, in 1939, they were forced to return to Vilkija to escape the encroaching Germans. By 1940, the Russians had taken over Lithuania and closed all the Jewish schools. Betty and her sister were separated from their family and eventually sent to a ghetto in Kovno where they nearly starved to death and lived in constant fear. Then the Nazis took control.

Within two years, almost half the Jews in the Kovno ghetto were gone. Betty managed to survive by volunteering to work in a German hospital laundry, where the work was hard but the food more plentiful. While there, she found a way to smuggle guns to the partisans through a nearby camp. Years later, she would meet a man in Israel who thanked her for having smuggled the gun he used to escape.

Ultimately, however, Betty was sent back to the ghetto in June 1944 and then to a concentration camp in Stutthof.

By 1945, the Nazis needed more labor in Germany, so they forced Betty and others from the camp to walk in a death march from Poland to Germany, accompanied by German guards with whips and guns. It was January. Betty and her sister ate snow to survive, occasionally passing dead bodies along the road. Late one night at a stop along the road, 17-year-old Betty made a decision that would save her life. Spotting the lights of a nearby village, Betty and several others slipped away from the march. There was nothing to lose.

Eventually, Betty and the other girls found a Polish woman who needed help on her farm. The girls promised to work, and the woman took them in. A month later, the war was coming to an end. But by then, as Betty learned, nearly all the Jews in Lithuania were killed, including most of her family. Betty was at a crossroads. Liberated by the Russian army on February 18, 1945, Betty had nowhere to go. She asked herself, "Who am I? Where do I belong in this world?" She then walked six kilometers to a nearby town where those in search of work gathered.

With no family or home to return to, Betty and five other "camp sisters" volunteered to work in a Russian hospital laundry. By fall of 1945, Betty, who was fluent in Russian, German, Lithuanian and Yiddish, found work as an interpreter. While this work was easier, Betty realized her future lay not with the Russians, but in the free world. So, with the help of fellow survivors, Betty escaped the Russians and ventured to Berlin.

That is how Betty Grossman ended up in that Berlin restaurant on October 10, 1945 talking with Isaac Goodfriend. She was 18, he was 21, yet each had lived a lifetime in the past five years. Immediately, a bond developed between them. In Isaac, Betty saw patience, personality, intelligence, and most importantly, "kindness in heart." And Isaac respected Betty's intellect and Orthodox Jewish upbringing, enjoyed her humor and admired her beauty. She was warm and caring. Within a month, they were very much in love. The two wrote a traditional letter of engagement, a t'naim, and set their wedding date for January 22, 1946.

Quickly, the young couple made preparations for a real simcha, a celebration of their love and survival. Isaac invited everyone he knew,

arranged for plenty of food and music, and rented a nightclub for the reception. Isaac and Betty's wedding was one of the first Jewish weddings in Berlin after the war ended. Almost 300 guests attended, and the reception lasted until 4 a.m.

The two set up an apartment in Berlin, but longed for stability and family. Betty had two surviving sisters, Pola in Munich, and Judy, the eldest, in Paris. Unable to reach Judy, Isaac and Betty united with Pola and her husband, Zundel, at the displaced person's (DP) camp in Feldafing. While the two couples formed a small, close family, Betty and Isaac were Zionists and longed to go to Palestine. Thinking it would be easier to get to Palestine from France, they spent several months trying to contact Judy in Paris and received an invitation from her in October 1946. Isaac, and then Betty, traveled to Paris and met Judy and her husband, Yisrael Kochavi.

In Paris, there was an Organization for Rehabilitation Through Training (ORT) school. Isaac enrolled in classes to be a mechanic, but soon changed to tailoring which would be more profitable. He purchased sewing machines, hired workers and, putting in 16-hour days, made up to 20 pairs of pants daily.

In February 1949, Betty gave birth to Serge Marcel, or Mark. At this point, Isaac's tailoring business was going well in Paris. But Isaac and Betty, with a new baby to raise, were more interested in moving to America, Canada, or Australia. Their old friend Aharon Saurymper suggested they move back to Berlin, because those in DP camps in Germany could get visas more quickly. So, in 1950, the couple returned to Berlin in search of something more.

It was in Berlin that Isaac first sang in front of a large group of people. On Pesach morning, at the synagogue in Rickestrasse where Isaac and Betty were attending services, the cantor had taken ill. There was no one to read the Torah or lead the service. Suddenly, the Gabbai looked over at Isaac and asked him to fill in for the cantor. Isaac nervously accepted. Hearing Isaac's beautiful baritone voice, a leader of the congregation approached Isaac afterwards and asked Isaac to be the congregation's new cantor. This was a turning point in Isaac and Betty's lives. For Isaac, "his heart opened to the meaning of the prayers when he expressed them with his voice. It felt glorious to sing." But Isaac never before thought it would be his life's work. Betty believed "the finger of God intervened at that moment." Isaac's beautiful voice, mind, and neshama, or soul, were finally recognized by others. Isaac had found his calling.

Isaac accepted the cantor position and quickly began music, piano, and voice lessons. Soon, Isaac, working in both East and West Berlin, became competent in his new profession. But the Goodfriends were still anxious to make a new beginning outside postwar Europe. So, like many other refugees seeking a better life, they applied for visas to both America and Canada. By late 1951, the family obtained visas to resettle in Canada. One month later, the Goodfriends boarded a ship called the Fair Sea to take them to their new home across the ocean.

The Jewish Immigrant Aid Service greeted Isaac, Betty, and Mark when they arrived in Montreal and gave the young family a room. To support his family, Isaac quickly took a job as a tailor. The pay was $35 a week, but the factory was a sweatshop. Isaac quit after a week. He yearned to be a cantor; Isaac believed this was God's plan. So Isaac began auditioning with local congregations. He was rejected several times, but after a private audition, was hired on the spot by the Shaare Zion Synagogue, a Conservative congregation of 1,400 families. It was March 1952, and Isaac had only stepped off the ship 10 weeks earlier. Isaac, now 27, accepted the position and quickly enrolled in the Conservatory of Music at McGill University and then in the French Conservatoire Provinciale to learn music theory and harmony. He also took private voice lessons. Their second son Enoch, named after Isaac's brother, was born in Montreal in 1953.

Professionally, Isaac blossomed for a time in Montreal. He gave a live radio performance for the French-Canadian Broadcast Company, accompanied by a large chamber orchestra. He performed in recitals sponsored by the French bishop and appeared in operas for the Provinciale and live television. Wanting more room to thrive professionally, Isaac first took a job with a Boston synagogue and then auditioned for the Community Temple in Cleveland, Ohio. Eager to start the next chapter in their lives, the Goodfriend family moved again, this time to Cleveland.

In 1957, there was a vibrant Jewish community in Cleveland. The Goodfriends were welcomed with open arms and immediately felt at home. Isaac was now the head cantor of a 700-family congregation. He had the opportunity to sing for Golda Meir and record Yiddish tunes for Jubilee Records.

Both Isaac and Betty joined a local Holocaust survivors group and helped create one of the first Holocaust memorials in the United States. Betty was active in both the congregation and the local chapter

of the Jewish National Fund. The family grew again with the birth of Isaac and Betty's third and youngest son, Perry, in 1959. Life was going well for the Goodfriends.

Isaac wanted greater responsibility and soon found it. He took the pulpit at the Ahavath Achim Synagogue in Atlanta, Georgia on October 29, 1965. In Atlanta, as they had in Cleveland, the couple became active in the local survivors organization and opened a new Jewish National Fund office. At the national level, Isaac became president of the Zionist Organization of America and was active in creating the U.S. Holocaust Memorial Museum in Washington, D.C.

In November 1976, Isaac's talent as a cantor and his many contributions to civic and Jewish life were formally recognized. Isaac was asked to sing the Star Spangled Banner at Jimmy Carter's Presidential inauguration. On January 20, 1977, the day Isaac turned 53, he stood on the steps of the Capitol and sang the National Anthem accompanied by the U.S. Marine Corps Band. Over 150 million people heard the voice of this Holocaust survivor who started out with nothing and reached such heights.

This was the pinnacle of Isaac's life. "I was like a man near the top of a ladder who has spent so much time stepping up that he has never looked down. . . . It was as if I chose that exact moment to look down the ladder at where I had come from, and to realize how precarious I felt. I had been so busy living my everyday life that I did not know how high I had climbed."

After 18 more years of professional and community service, Isaac retired in 1995 at the age of 71. To this day, Isaac and Betty Goodfriend remain active in community service organizations at the local and national level. Yet, through all their achievements and commitments to do for others, Isaac and Betty have never forgotten their childhoods, their families, their Eastern European Jewish way of life, all destroyed in the Holocaust.

Looking back on his life, Isaac feels he has traveled a world away from where he was during his war-ravaged youth. He "somehow managed to build a bridge between two distinct lives: the ashes from whence I came and the heights to which I soared. God gave me a chance. He gave me life. He gave me another 60 or 70 years."

Isaac continues, "Now that I look upon my survival, I know that my being saved by an unknown supernatural force involved faith, fate, a miracle, or all three. The same fate and faith that kept me alive provided me with opportunities to fulfill my dreams, achieve my goals, and reach all that I aspired to accomplish. But I realize now how short life is and how much there is left to accomplish. I have to talk fast, and quickly tell future generations while I still have the breath to do so."

Betty still remembers her terrifying experiences growing up, yet looks forward to the future. "The memories can't be erased or turned off," she declares, "But, the 'remnants of the remnants' must remember and speak up. Don't give up, don't give in. Carry on with dignity and trust in God. Be kind to your fellow human beings. Be yourself and work for a good world for you, your family, and future generations. To have a good name and be well-respected are better than riches. Never forget what one human being can accomplish or destroy. Don't be ashamed. Be proud. Always look up and ahead."

henry friedman

the tallis is my shield

As a child growing up in Romania in the early 20th century, Henry Friedman had a comfortable life and a happy childhood. His parents were very assimilated Jews. His father was an insurance broker and his mother a housewife. Henry and his brother and sister enjoyed a family vacation once a year. However, as in other Eastern European countries, there was a great deal of anti-Semitism. According to Henry, "It happened even in the olden days. We had to secure our home by locking the front gate. If there was a drought, they'd blame the Jews, and if there was too much rain, they would blame the Jews. We just got used to it. They would come from the university to break windows and throw rocks. No one defended the Jews; therefore, we were very easy to blame."

When Henry, or Imre as he was called then, was born in 1923, Oradea-Mare, the city in Transylvania where he lived, was considered part of Romania. During the early part of World War II, it became part of Hungary. Hungary was one of the last countries that Germany invaded; their forces entered the country on March 19, 1944. Prior to the German invasion, Hungary was one of Germany's allies, not one of the countries that it had conquered. As an ally, Hungary issued anti-

Semitic legislation, but did not go as far as the Nazis' genocide. The Nazis, frustrated that Hungary would not surrender control of its Jews, took over Hungary, replacing its dictator with a German collaborator. The Nazis then began to deport Jews from Hungary to the concentration camps at the rate of 12,000 Jews daily. Additionally, a new law was passed requiring all Jews to wear yellow stars.

During Nazi rule, Henry's life became difficult. At 21 years old, he was drafted into the army, and his brother and father were conscripted for forced labor. Life was very hard, especially since Henry's father had never done any physical labor. "With draft notice in my back pocket, and coat and backpack, I kissed my family goodbye, not knowing that I would never see them again," Henry sadly recalls. Before he left for the army, his grandmother took him to the other side of the duplex where they lived for what appeared to be a prearranged meeting with a white haired old man wearing a tallit. The man placed the tallit across Henry's shoulders, laid his hands on Henry's head, and blessed him. At that moment, Henry did not put much thought into the unusual encounter and, in fact, would not think about it again until after the war. Today, however, Henry declares that with that blessing, he received a shield of protection that kept him safe both throughout the Holocaust and even up until today. On three separate occasions Henry fervently believes this blessing kept him alive.

In the army, Henry was sent to a huge factory in Budapest that made planes and tanks for the German army. He had studied at the university and was familiar with machinery. He worked there for two months from May until July. He remembers, "There were air raids every day. I ran to the shelter, but I was told that there was no room for Jews."

One day, he was waiting in line for hot soup when a Hungarian captain in charge of the entire factory of 100,000 workers stopped in front of him. Pointing at Henry, he shouted, "Jew, a part of your star is not sewn on perfectly. Go to my office now." Following Henry into the office, the captain beat him badly. Henry recalls with a shudder, "He was a sadist. When he hit me, he had a smirk on his face." A few days later, the captain found out where Henry was working in the foundry, and while Henry was pouring the molten steel into forms, he picked up an iron rod and hit Henry in the back. The sparks from the rod burned through Henry's clothes. Finally, when Henry could no longer endure the torture, he showed the scar with pus running down it to his direct supervisor and explained, "I have an infection and don't want to make others sick."

Henry's mural of Theodore Herzl

Henry was then sent to a military hospital and assigned a number. While he was waiting for treatment, the hospital was bombed and reduced to flaming rubble. After this horrific incident, he was transported 250 miles west to another military hospital. Fortunately, conditions were very good there. A major said to him, "Son, I know who you are and why you are here. We're having heavy casualties, however, and we need to send you back to your unit."

Luckily, the sadistic Hungarian captain had given up looking for him. Henry learned that a Swedish representative, Raoul Wallenberg, was issuing Swedish passports that protected Jews waiting to immigrate to Sweden. The Hungarians honored the passports, but the Nazis would not. Henry found out about the passports and obtained one from the Swedish consulate, hoping that it would be useful in the future. At that time, the Russians had surrounded Budapest, and Henry sought refuge in a stable. There was no food or water, and one day while he scavenged for food, the Nazis recaptured him.

Henry was forced to climb to the top of mountains in Budapest to bring food to German soldiers in the middle of the night in the freezing cold winter. In addition Henry had to bring dead or wounded German soldiers down to the base of the mountain to a temporary hospital. While he was carrying wounded German soldiers, he was hit by shrapnel and was in danger of bleeding or freezing to death; however, he slid down the mountain of snow and snuck into a Hungarian civilian hospital. There, doctors removed the fragments of shrapnel. He returned to the Germans because the Hungarians, fearing for their own safety, could not keep him long, and when the Germans saw his bandage, they told him they were taking him to a German hospital. Actually, they took him to a cemetery along with three other wounded Jews, where he faced a gun barrel. The Nazi soldiers lined up the Jews and shot them. Fortunately, the bullet only grazed Henry, but they left him for dead. Unconscious until morning, he realized upon waking that he survived the cold night because two other bodies had fallen on top of him and kept him warm.

When he left the cemetery, he returned to the Hungarian civilian hospital, entered through a side entrance, and hid under a heap of coal. After seven days of hiding, Henry needed food. He found frozen fried chicken covered in mold in the hospital morgue, and it lasted him 10 days. Finally the Russians arrived and Henry felt safe enough to climb up to the main room where he was treated for leg wounds. He made his own crutches. Marching this time with Russians guards, he found himself walking down a street with people lined up in columns on both sides of the sidewalk. A young woman motioned to him from the sidewalk. "I felt under a hypnotic trance and began to walk towards her," Henry explains. She told me to get lost; that this marching group was going to Siberia. By the time Henry realized what she was saying, she had disappeared. The entire column passed him by, and he ran past pushcarts to the other side of the river. He asked for directions to the train station because he wanted to go home. Henry remembers walking all day until it was dark. A stranger appeared and invited him to spend the night . At this stranger's house, Henry received a warm meal, and a place to sleep. It was then that Henry learned that his home was no longer located in Romania but rather in Hungary. In the morning Henry awoke to find that this man had sewn a Hungarian armband – red, yellow and blue for him. This armband would protect him on his way home. He took Henry to the train station where the Red Cross had set up tables. When they saw Henry wearing the Hungarian armband, they gave him a train ticket to return home. When Henry arrived at his house, he knocked on the door of his childhood home. Strangers answered the door, and although Henry could see his family's furniture inside, he was told that this was not his house and to go away.

He went to the local hospital and saw other Jews from his town who had survived. There was a bulletin that said his brother was on his way home, and Henry joyfully prepared for his arrival. Later, someone told him that it couldn't be his brother because his brother had been sick with typhus and shot. When he heard this news, he couldn't stop crying. The Gentiles couldn't understand the Jews' sadness, believing it to be an exaggeration; they didn't understand his pain. He recalls these empty days. "We survivors weren't like humans anymore. Never sleeping. Never eating. Just fear and exhaustion. We didn't even really understand what was going on. When you would touch another person, that human contact would make them jump."

Henry knew that to maintain his sanity he would have to start all over some place new. He planned ahead to travel to the nearest big port in Italy and take an ocean liner to escape Eastern Europe. He went to Italy where he spent five years painting portraits and murals . While living in Milan, he saw the movie Gone with the Wind. He saw all that was dear to Scarlett had been destroyed by war and was reminded of the parallels to his own life. At the time, he thought Atlanta, Georgia was a fictitious place, but ironically, he soon moved there.

In May 1950, he immigrated to America, specifically, Atlanta. Mickey Eisenberg, a social worker for the Atlanta Jewish Federation, arranged for his sponsorship. He worked as a house painter. Henry worked as a house painter for a year and a half before being hired by the Progressive Club, a private Jewish social club. The club offered kinship and community that he desperately needed. He married his wife Sherry, celebrating their reception at the club. Sherry and Henry have one son, Steven, whom they named after his brother.

Henry learned about the food industry, eventually becoming the head buyer of CFS Continental. SYSCO Foods purchased CFS, and Henry became the non-edible products merchandiser. He retired from the industry in 1992.

The memory of the tallit blessing has been a constant inspiration to Henry to live his life to the fullest while never forgetting his past.

ben walker

lion of judah

He escaped from the death and destruction of the Holocaust and found his way to Kibbutz Nitzanim in Eretz Yisrael, the land of milk and honey. He was no longer a Jew of the shtetl, weak and afraid; he was a bold and proud Jew living in Israel, a lion of Judah, given a second chance at life.

Ben Walker was born as Benjamin Walzer in Czernowitz, in the Bukovina region of Romania, on January 16, 1935. He lived with his parents and younger sister in the small town of Nepolocauti. His grandparents, four uncles, and an aunt all lived on a large farm nearby. "I had a fine time at the farm, riding horses and climbing cherry trees," Ben remembers. But the good life soon came to end.

"When the war started, it interrupted my Jewish education and Jewish life," he said. In 1941, when Germany invaded Russia, the Nazis left Romania, with its pro-Nazi government, to dispose of its own Jews.

Later that year, Ben's family was deported east to Transnistria. First, they were put in a ghetto in Mogilev, and then they had to march on foot to Kopaigorod where, separated now from their relatives, they were forced to live in a barn with almost 50 families. This was

Romania's way of killing its Jews - they were crowded into barns and left to die slowly of starvation, cold and disease. No one could run away because their families would all be hanged; no one would help them, and the forests were full of wild animals. The prisoners had to bury their own dead in shallow graves. Animals would come and dig up the bodies. A strange thing took place; the healthy people died faster than the sick ones. This was possible, Ben says, because the sick people had been used to disease all their lives, while those who were healthy had no resistance to the new onslaught..

A year later, in the cold winter of 1942, Ben's father and younger sister died from the horrible conditions. Ben, now 7, was sick with typhus. There wasn't much to eat—a family could eat soup made from a scrap of potato. It was only through this minimal nourishment, coupled with his mother's love, that Ben survived.

Children left without parents were sent to an orphanage near Kopaigorod, and Ben's mother, afraid he would have no one to take care of him if she died, managed to get him in. He was much happier and healthier there, away from the misery of the barn. "I was taught to sing . . . we had performances and regular meals," Ben fondly remembers. Later, when conditions improved at the barn, and she was able to travel into the village to work, Ben's mother got him back.

In spring of 1944, as the war drew closer to an end, the Romanians retreated from Transnistria. Ben and his mother returned home by hitchhiking on a train shipping ammunition for the advancing Russian army. "If the Luftwaffe had dropped one little bomb on that train, we would have been dead meat," Ben recalls.

Arriving at their doorstep, they found strangers had occupied their house. Traveling next to his grandparents' farm, they found the Communists had taken it over. Everyone had perished, except for Ben's aunt and two uncles, one now in Siberia. Ben and his mother then went to live with a non-Jewish family, good friends of his grandfather's. Ben's mother found an old postcard showing the address of her husband's brother and sister in the United States, whom she didn't know much about. They wrote to them, and their relatives began to send them food, including sacks of flour and cornmeal, with $10 and $20 bills hidden inside. Ben states, "This money was very valuable because the American dollar was king." At great risk, the little-known aunt and uncle had become Ben's lifeline.

When Ben reached 13 in 1948, he became a bar mitzvah, but life kept getting worse for the Jews. He and a friend once were chased by an anti-Semitic mob, and only escaped by jumping in a river. As Romania became increasingly Communist, they knew they had to immigrate to America or Israel. At that time, Romania saw the United States as an enemy, so it was dangerous to ask for permission to go there. "We would lose our job, property, and maybe even our life. People who chose to go to the United States disappeared all the time," Ben remembers. However, Romania did allow its Jews to go to Israel as a way of getting rid of them.

Ben and his mother immigrated to Israel in 1951. The trip, in an overcrowded ship leaving a Black Sea port, was miserable, but after four days, they arrived in Israel to a wonderful welcome. "People threw oranges at us in welcome. I had never seen an orange. I went to the top of the boat and collected them."

Ben was sent to Kibbutz Nitzanim, in the Negev near the Gaza border. His mother went to a moshav, a collective farm, in Tzofit to live with her brother, who had escaped from Siberia. Life on the kibbutz was one of the best experiences of Ben's life, even though at first he saw Israel as a desert compared to lush Romania. He was one of 30 teenagers, almost all of them Romanian survivors of the Holocaust. There, the pain of Europe was forgotten. It was almost as though there was a silent agreement never to discuss that aspect of their lives. It wasn't important to Ben. "Your experience in the shtetl of being afraid, of anti-Semitism and hatred, is gone. This was a new life," he says. "It was a welcome start for me. What I lost I didn't want to be reminded of. We were new Jews, proud Israelis. Not afraid, from the anti-Semitism of the shtetl. We were the lions of Judah."

Smiling, Ben explains, "We worked hard and studied hard, and every evening we sang and danced. We were close as teenagers. It gave me a new perspective. After the suffering of war, this was a liberation. I was back on a farm, in the fields, with nature. I wasn't locked up. I wasn't threatened. It gave me a new life. I came out of the dead, so to speak."

Ben recalls one experience in particular on the kibbutz in which he was hailed as a hero. Kibbutz Nitzanim, on the border, had many conflicts with neighboring Arabs. For several weeks, a few sheep each day disappeared. One day Ben, after returning the sheep from their pasture to the corral, left his lunch bag behind and went back to retrieve it. Reaching the corral, he saw something puzzling; the gate was open and the sheep were walking out.

"I ran as fast as I could and called the kibbutz security officer," Ben declared. They returned in a jeep with a machine gun, looked in a nearby wadi and saw four sheep there. Two of the "sheep" raised their hands in the air! Arabs had donned sheepskin in order to lead the sheep out of the pasture. "I was a big hero, of course. We were famous for solving the mystery," he proudly recalls.

His mother, following Jewish law, married her brother-in-law Harry Walker and immigrated to the United States. Ben, now 18, remained in Israel and entered the army. Basic training was an extreme challenge, and Ben didn't know if we would make it through, but he did and considered it a worthwhile achievement. He became an instructor and then a sergeant in charge of 25 men and saw combat near the border in 1955.

Ben wanted to stay in Israel, but his mother wanted him to come to the United States, and, realizing he needed to go to college, he obliged. He arrived in Florida on August 19, 1956. "I came to Port Canaveral at night, with the lights shining along Miami Beach."

"I only knew two words: 'water' and 'thank you,' " admits Ben. He soon learned English , assisted by his home television set, and passed the GED exam to receive his diploma. He went to Orlando Junior College while teaching afternoon Hebrew school at a synagogue. Tutoring children was an opportunity Ben truly enjoyed, and his experience in Israel gave him a good perspective from which to teach them. He then went on to the University of Florida in Gainesville, where he studied math education and helped start the first Hebrew school at a growing synagogue there as well. After graduating, he went to Tampa where he spent five years teaching junior high school math in a public school and Hebrew at a local Hebrew school.

With the Cold War heating up, and not many Americans able to speak Russian, Ben decided to study the language at the University of South Florida in Tampa, where he was his professor's only student. When the professor had taught him all the Russian he could, Ben went to Syracuse University and received a degree in Russian.

Meanwhile, he met a woman whose parents had also come from Czernowitz, escaped Romania and gone to Chile. The young woman, Ruth Tennenbaum, had studied English in Chile and now was coming to Indiana on a Fulbright scholarship. Ben's mother had told him about her, and Ben, after speaking to her many times on the telephone, invited her to visit him in Orlando. Before long they were married.

He was offered an educational position in Chattanooga, and they moved there. In 1967, their daughter Ronit was born, and, two years later, their daughter Naomi. A new synagogue in Atlanta, Temple Sinai, hired Ben as its educational director. In 1982, Ben made a career change and became an insurance salesman. By 1984, he was buying and selling real estate. Ben's wife Ruth teaches Spanish at The Weber High School, a Jewish high school in Atlanta. Today Ben is semi-retired. He often is asked to speak about the Holocaust at the Breman Jewish Heritage Museum. Most of all he enjoys playing with his grandchild.

Mr. Walker never spoke of his Holocaust experiences to his children. He was not proud of the Holocaust, as the Jews were unable to defend themselves from persecution. He wanted to forget the oppressed Jews of Europe and to take pride in the brave Israeli soldiers who defend the Jewish homeland.

Today, he realizes the younger generation must understand what happened during those terrible years of Transnistria's "forgotten Holocaust." He can see that violence still takes its bloody toll upon the world, as evidenced by the suicide bombings in Israel.

"After 9/11 in 2001, I realized I'm getting older, and suddenly there was a wakeup call to America that we are not terribly loved in this world. There is evil again, like the suicide bombers. And I said, well, this is almost history repeating itself. I will tell the younger generation. They should know similar events took place on a much larger scale in Europe in World War II. We didn't stop evil. It continued to grow and grow. We'll soon be gone. It's time for them to learn the Holocaust was real."

shelly weiner

spared by the kindness of strangers

After many terrifying months of hiding in a hayloft, Shelly Weiner's mother Eva lost her will to carry on. "Don't you want to see me dance under my chuppah?" pleaded 5-year-old Shelly. "They won't catch us!" Although starving and exhausted, the vision of her little daughter one day marrying under a chuppah, a marriage canopy, nourished Eva's will to carry on and remain in hiding from the Nazis.

In the summer of 1941, the Nazis invaded Rovno, in eastern Poland. The persecution of the Jews began slowly. Jews were banned from markets, and then they were required to obey curfews. Shelly was forced to grow up even though she was only 4 years old. The Germans called the men in her family to work, but her grandfather learned this order was actually a trick to get them to go obediently to concentration camps. Her grandfather built a hiding place in the house for the men. It was Shelly and her cousin's job to play in the yard and watch for Nazis and to warn the men to hide quickly if they came.

The nightmare got worse. Rovno was turned into a ghetto, and the family was moved into a single room with many strangers. "The women were separated from the men. I never saw my grandfather

again," Shelly recalls with distress. "We had a cheerful house before, and this was dreary. We were only fed once a day. And there was nothing to do."

One night after they'd been there three months, a Gentile neighbor tipped off Shelly's mother that the Jews of Rovno were about to be killed. Shelly's mother woke her, and together they snuck out of the ghetto to her aunt's village nearby. The very next day in Rovno, 15,000 Jews were taken to the outskirts of town and killed. "There were 25,000 Jews in Rovno before the war and only about 100 after," Shelly explains.

Shelly, her mother, her cousin Rachel, and her aunt Sonia had to hide. They squeezed into a hayloft belonging to a Gentile man. He had a wife and a 12-year-old daughter and was worried about risking his family by hiding Jews. But he also had an 18-year-old son who, with his friends, had traveled to town to help the Poles clean up their "action" and earn some money. Upon arriving, the young men found that the work involved throwing the dead men, women and children into the ditches. The farmer's son was so repulsed by what he saw that he and his friends decided to join the Resistance and fight the Germans. More importantly, he convinced his father to hide Shelly and her family.

The Gentile family was good to them, but the two mothers and their two young daughters could rarely leave the hayloft – only twice in a year and a half, although it was bitterly cold in the winter and full of rats and lice. "To keep us busy, our mothers would talk to us. We would make small animals out of the straw. It was better than a ghetto or a death camp," Shelly recalls.

Once they had to hide in another farmer's attic after they were nearly discovered because Shelly's crying had almost given them away. The attic was so cold that when the farmer came to get them down one day, Shelly had no pulse. She remembers, "I could hear [the people around me] talking about how they thought I was dead and wondering how they'd bury me because the ground was frozen. They rubbed me with snow and revived me." Shelly, her mother, her aunt and cousin immediately returned to the hayloft for safety.

Another time Shelly recalls hallucinating and shouting at random. The family was afraid this behavior would lead to their discovery. It turned out she was suffering from malnutrition, a lack of protein, because she wouldn't eat the rabbit stew they were offered. One of the farmers found something for her to eat, and she got better.

In the summer of 1943, Shelly and her family were forced to move when someone tipped off the Nazis about their hiding. It was too risky to keep them in the hayloft. At this moment, Shelly's mother thought their lives were over. The farmer was ordered to turn them over to Ukrainian SS troops who were searching for hidden Jews. "Our mothers said, 'Give us a few minutes to say goodbye to each other.' Then the farmer left, and my cousin and I pleaded with our moms, 'Let's not just go down and give ourselves up, but run to the woods.' We asked them, 'Wouldn't you want to take us to the chuppah?'" The passionate girls' pleas convinced their mothers to choose life over death, so they ran away to the forest together. "We could hear dogs in the forest and people calling for us. By some miracle, something diverted their attention," Shelly remembers. They stayed hidden overnight. Standing on his roof, peering into the forest, the farmer spotted the frightened four and retrieved them. Their lives still in danger, Shelly's family hid in the wheat fields without food or water for three days. Once again, one of the kind farmers concealed them, first underneath a horse trough and then in a hole in the ground that he used to hide grain from the pilfering Germans. The hole was damp; it was dark and rat infested, and Shelly had to crawl on her belly to retrieve food and water. Aunt Sonia became ill, and Shelly later developed pneumonia and typhoid fever. "We were there for eight months. I remember it being very dark. To this day, I still enjoy the sun very much," she explains.

In 1944, the Russians liberated that part of Poland. One day, the farmer took Shelly's mom and aunt into town to see if it was safe for them to return home. It was. They went back to their house where Shelly and Aunt Sonia eventually recovered.

Rovno was now part of the Soviet Union, and Shelly's mother was being pressured to become a Communist. They left and went to Poland. In Poland, they found Shelly's father and together traveled to a displaced person's camp near Munich. They lived in DP camps, mainly one in Poking, for three years. "My mother and father wanted to escape to Israel, but it was too dangerous" because it was illegal for Jewish refugees to immigrate to Israel. The Red Cross kept telephone books for all major American cities, so Shelly's father went to the Red Cross to locate relatives in America. "My father wrote to every Jacob or Louis Weiner in the phone book – 500 or 600 [individually typed] letters! Eventually, he did contact my uncle who sponsored us," Shelly recalls.

Shelly and her parents arrived in New York on Columbus Day 1949. They moved to Philadelphia where there weren't very many other immigrants. Her original name, Rachel, was Americanized to Rochelle and later to Shelly. "I was in 7th grade and didn't know English. I didn't look like the other American girls. I had hand-me-down clothes and long braids and didn't like American food. But eventually I learned to adjust."

Years later, Shelly married Frank Weiner, whose last name was the same by coincidence. They had three children. Although they wanted to move to the South where life was slower, they knew it was important that their kids grow up in a Jewish environment, so they chose Greensboro, North Carolina, where there was a Jewish day school. When her children were older, Shelly returned to school. She worked for a child abuse program and also had her own tropical plant business. Her husband owned restaurants and now has an import-export business.

When Shelly's family left Poland in 1949, they lost track of Aunt Sonia and cousin Rachel. "In the 1960s, my mother went to Israel. She met someone on the street who told her that her sister was in Russia. In 1974, we went to Russia and found my aunt. We spent three weeks there and had to get special permission to stay in their home. If they ever wanted to leave, we said we'd help them," explains Shelly. Sonia and her daughter Rachel, immigrated to the United States in 1980, eventually settling in Greensboro near Shelly. "They're the only close family I have left," she admits.

And what became of the hayloft farmer's family, the ones who risked their own lives to save the lives of four others? Although the farmer's family was spared persecution for hiding Jews, their 18-year-old son was captured and killed by Germans three months before liberation. The farmer and his wife died shortly thereafter. Their daughter lived on the farm for years, and Shelly and her mother sent regular "thank you" packages for the rest of her life.

Since coming to America, Shelly has been involved in Holocaust education. Her latest project is with the Joint Distribution Committee where Greensboro is paired with a sister city in Moldova. Shelly and other Greensboro volunteers work to teach the Jewish citizens of Moldova about their Jewish background. Sending teachers and rabbis, running a summer camp for families and raising money to restore the cemetery are some of the ways they do so. Under Communism, the Jews of Moldova had not been exposed to their religion, their culture, and their heritage for many years.

Survivors feel a tremendous guilt, Shelly explains. "We have to do so much more than others to make up for lost lives. We can only start with the people around us."

By the way, Shelly and Frank had a very proper Jewish wedding, with a chuppah. Her mother was there. And she even danced at their wedding.

until next sunday

Manuela Bornstein couldn't take swimming lessons, sit on a park bench, shop during the day – simply because she was Jewish. In a suburb of Paris, France in 1942, Jews possessed few rights. Soon after these harsh laws were passed, Jews also had to wear a yellow star on their jackets. In school, Manuela recalls wearing a suit that her mother had made for her complete with its bold yellow star. Her teacher asked her to get her jacket from the hallway and showed everyone the coat. She explained that some people were prejudiced against Jews, but that the class should be nice to Manuela and not tease her. Sixty-one years later, Manuela remembers this teacher, Madame Bargain, as a great woman. This teacher was very courageous, as one of the children could have told that story to their parents, who could have denounced her to the Gestapo. She truly took a chance.

Before the regulations against Jews were put in place, Manuela lived with her mother, father and younger sister in an apartment near Paris. Her father was a businessman who imported and exported food, and her mother was a housewife. She was almost seven when the Germans invaded in 1940. Soon after, her father's company deteriorated. Eventually, he wasn't allowed to own it anymore. He sold it, relegated

to a position in the company's background. Jews could not own a car, so he had to ride his bicycle to work, or, if he rode the subway, he had to ride in a section reserved for Jews. Manuela's mother feared for her husband every day he went to work as it was common for Jews to disappear and never be heard from again. In 1941, Manuela's maternal grandmother, whom her father had been unable to convince to leave Germany, committed suicide, seeing nothing but a tragic future for Jews. However, Manuela's mother told her that if her grandmother had come to Paris to live with them, perhaps they would not have been able to escape as they did.

In July 1942, the Germans rounded up all the Jews in Paris and surrounding areas. At 3 and 4 a.m., the Nazis banged on the doors with their guns and their boots, and took people within. Amazingly, the Germans passed by their door. "Why they didn't come for us, I'll never know," says Manuela. This was a wake-up call for Manuela's parents who realized that they had to leave Paris as soon as possible. Manuela's father was Dutch, and the Dutch community put the family in contact with two teenagers working for the Resistance who helped them flee to the free part of southern France.

When the family fled their house, they left empty-handed so that nobody would suspect they were escaping. They walked to the apartment of Catholic friends, ate dinner with them; then the father of that family lit the furnace and burned their Jewish stars. Heading to the train station, the family received tickets from two young men who worked for the Resistance. However, the train stood motionless for a long time, and Manuela's parents grew increasingly nervous. (Manuela's mother gave both daughters each a poison pill so that if the Germans caught them, they could swallow the pill and end their lives without suffering.) They did not know what the hold-up was about but later learned that other Jews were being rounded up on the train next to them. When the train lurched forward, they breathed a sigh of relief.

The family disembarked from the train just north of the line separating Nazi-controlled France and free France. At night, they crossed the demarcation line. One teenager propped the children on his bicycle, while the parents ran behind. Manuela's mother later told her how she wore a pink slip and a blue suit that night and that eventually from her nervous sweat, the slip turned blue. They paid the young men who risked their lives and were greeted by the French army who welcomed them with dinner and a bed. The next morning they made their way to the next large city, Perigueux.

Despite the army's warm welcome, Manuela's parents were forced to report to the police for illegally crossing the lines of demarcation. Although they weren't allowed to remain in Perigueux, they were allowed to move within 35 miles. After three weeks, they found a tiny apartment, one without running water, to rent in the town of Le Got. The girls had to pump water from across the street at a railroad station and carry it back to the apartment.

People in Le Got knew the Mendelses were Jewish refugees, and the mayor of the adjoining town was a remarkable man who worked for the resistance. He managed to get a job for Manuela's father and fake identification cards for both of her parents. They never knew

when a round-up was going to occur, so her father often spent a day or night hiding in the forest. Her parents could go out only on Saturday. Each Sunday, they toasted one another, "Jusqu'au dimanche prochain" – until next Sunday. They never knew what lay ahead.

In 1943, while they were in Le Got, Manuela's brother was born. Her parents named him Franklin, after United States President Franklin Delano Roosevelt. If he had been a girl, they would have named him Marianne, after the symbol of French freedom. In 1944, Paris was liberated, and the Mendels returned to their apartment in Paris. Through the Red Cross, Manuela's family sadly learned that most of their relatives had died during the war. Manuela's sister, Jacqueline, married and moved to the United States from France.

When Manuela came to the United States in 1960, she traveled to San Francisco to visit her Dutch cousins, who had moved there after the war. Friends set her up with a man who knew the area well, Murray Bornstein, a civil engineer. Eventually they married and moved to Hawaii for a year. "Hawaii was wonderful," recalls Manuela, "but we were big city people." She worked as a travel agent, a career she pursued for 35 years. Eventually, they moved back to the mainland, returning to San Francisco. Although Manuela's parents joined them in 1962, they were never comfortable in America and they moved back to France in 1972. Later Murray's company transferred him to Atlanta, where Manuela now resides.

Her husband has since died, but Manuela is happy in Atlanta. She is a violinist with the Atlanta Community Symphony Orchestra and has spoken at the William Breman Jewish Heritage Museum, Hadassah, and at the Shoah Foundation about her experiences during the Holocaust. She has two sons, Jack and Nathaniel, and three grandchildren.

Her message to future generations is to "reach out, keep your eyes open, be grateful and learn as much as you can." Manuela cares a great deal about her family. She is close to her sister and calls her every morning on her way to work. She encourages today's youth to write down everything, including their family history. In this way, they can stay educated and learn about their past. She also believes in the importance of connecting with people who do not share our heritage. She explains, "We tend to attach ourselves to people like us, but it is good to reach out to others unlike ourselves, so they can see the ridiculousness of discrimination."

albert baron

winter trek through the pyrenees

Just a boy of 8, Albert Baron struggled through the massive heaps of snow and blinding wind as his family trekked through the Pyrenees Mountains. Albert recalls climbing through the mountains with his family and two others. Led by hired Basque guides, his father had determined that during this storm, German soldiers would never think anyone would attempt the climb.

Albert was born in Nancy, France, 150 miles east of Paris. He lived in a town of roughly 60,000 people of whom perhaps 5,000 were Jewish. His family was Conservative, although his family didn't keep kosher; in fact, few families did. It was not the type of Jewish community that one might find in Eastern Europe; very few were Orthodox.

In 1940, the family's peaceful existence ended when Germany invaded France. Nancy, near the German border, was one of the first cities the Germans bombed. At 6, Albert remembers a bomb falling in his family's courtyard, spraying shrapnel near where his sister was sleeping. After the bombing, everyone was sent to air raid shelters for two weeks; food was scarce and water minimal.

In Nancy, his father was a custom tailor for men's and women's

clothes. "It was a successful little business," Albert says. "Thankfully, that's how we were able to escape. He had the money. There were two trains of thought. Some people didn't want to leave because they didn't want to leave their businesses. Others, like my dad, were smart. He said, 'Let's get out of here.' "

Albert's father bought a truck, and the family took whatever they could and fled for Toulouse in what they called "Free France." There, the Germans had control, but put in a French puppet government called the Vichy government. The Barons still were not safe. The Vichy government was rounding up Jews, and Albert's parents were targets because they were not French citizens. He doesn't know why they never sought citizenship. "I'll never figure that one out," Albert ponders.

Initially, the family hid in an attic in Toulouse, but the French Gestapo chased Albert's father, so the family escaped into the Pyrenees and rented a small villa at the foothills of the mountains. "We had somewhat of a normal life there," Albert recalls. The family lived in a small town in the mountains and had a garden to provide them with food. They rode horses, went skiing at a nearby ski resort called Luchon, and he learned to read and write Hebrew from a rabbi. One day, when Albert was walking to school, he spotted two German soldiers on the side of the street. His father had shown him pictures of French and German soldiers, explaining the difference. After this incident, his father decided to move once again for the family's safety.

First, the children were placed in a monastery for three weeks. They were treated well, given food, and were very thankful to the monks who risked their lives to help Jews. When the time was right to leave, Albert's parents came for them. With two other families, they made the journey through the Pyrenees Mountains.

The Basque guides told Albert's father the Germans probably wouldn't catch them; there was too much snow and it was almost Christmas. "Who would be crazy enough to be out there in the middle of winter?" the guides assured them. The snow, in some places, was over his head, Albert recalls. The adults would make a path, and the children would follow. The trip took 24 hours, and the family was told they couldn't stop for more than a few minutes at a time, or they'd get frostbite. It was harder on the adults, Albert thinks. "I probably had more stamina." They were warmly dressed, including ski masks. "My dad being a tailor, he made sure we had the right clothes."

Albert's only family possession

The most dangerous part of the trip, for them, was the first half, going up the mountains; once they got to the top, they were in Spain. But for their guides, it was the opposite. As they approached the frontier and saw a Spanish border patrol, their guides fled, fearing they'd be thrown in jail in Spain since the Basques had been on the losing side of the recent Spanish Civil War.

Once the Barons arrived in Barcelona, Spain, there was some peace in their lives. Still, it was hard for them at first. Albert's father was not allowed to work and money was scarce. Although Albert's aunt lived in America, the United States refused to extend a visa to the Barons. Canada, however, allowed 5,000 Jews to enter, and Albert's father was eager to leave Europe. With the help of the Hebrew Immigration Aid Society, Albert's family sailed on a Portuguese freighter bound for Philadelphia and then on a train to Montreal, Canada in 1944.

Life wasn't easy for the Barons, new immigrants with only $12 to feed a family of four. Albert's parents shortly went into business; his mother worked as a seamstress and his father as a custom tailor. For a long time, it was tough for Albert. Defensive against anti-Semitic remarks, he got into a lot of fights. Only when his family moved into an area mostly inhabited by Jews did things become better. During a Young Men's Hebrew Association fair, he noticed a girl about his age. The young woman, Rita, invited him to her 17th birthday party. Albert and Rita have been married for 48 years and have two children, Barbara and Mark.

Albert and his family moved to Atlanta in 1970 where he worked for a large chemical company called Zep Manufacturing Co. as director of national sales. He retired in 1996. He has returned to France numerous times but was upset to see that his home is no longer there. In its place is a 20-story building.

Reflecting on his Holocaust experience, Albert emphasizes the importance of family. He questions why God allowed so many people to die, but is proud nonetheless to be a Jew. "Live in peace and harmony, and have concern for Israel and the Jewish people," he stresses. His experience, he says, made him a Zionist, and he was also active with the Anti-Defamation League. "Anti-Semitism is the reason we have Israel. People don't realize that if we had had a country called Israel when the war started, a million or two million people would have been saved."

herbert kohn

i have tried to remove hate from my vocabulary

When Herbert Kohn returned to Germany as an 18-year-old GI, he was disappointed that the war ended two days later. He hadn't had a chance to fight the nation which had persecuted him and his family. However, when he traveled to Germany decades later, he realized that vengeance would serve no purpose.

Herbert was born on September 27, 1926 in Frankfurt-am-Main, Germany. His family, which traced their roots in Germany back to 1490, thought of themselves as Jewish Germans, not as German Jews. His father and both his grandfathers had fought for Germany in World War I, and one of his grandfathers had been the first Jewish major in the Kaiser's army. However, the Kohns' proud German heritage would soon be tested.

When Herbert was 6 and in first grade, Hitler came to power, and a month later, the persecution of the Jews began. Herbert's teacher asked if there were any Jews in class. Herbert proudly answered, "Yes." The teacher then said that he had to leave as Jews were not allowed in public school any longer. It was very traumatic, and young Herbert walked home alone.

The laws and rules against the Jews quickly became harsher and

harsher. Herbert was sent to a segregated school relegated for Jews. Soon, signs of increased anti-Semitism were everywhere. Jews could not sit on park benches. Jews could not eat at restaurants. Jews were forced to obey curfews, and Jews were required to have a "J" on identity cards, and later, a Jewish star on their outer clothing.

"For the first three or four years, my father thought all of that would go away," Herbert explains. In time, however, his father realized that the climate of anti-Semitism was reaching a fevered pitch, and he knew that they must escape Germany. Searching frantically, they found willing relatives, Dora and Mervin Sterne in Birmingham, Alabama, to sponsor them and received visas. Unfortunately, U.S. immigration laws wouldn't let them come until 1940. They were stuck in Germany.

Then, on November 9, 1938, the Kristallnacht riots shattered any illusions for the Jews. A Storm Trooper invaded the Kohn home. Pushing Herbert's mother to the ground, the Storm Trooper arrested his father who was taken with most of the adult male Jews in the community. Outside, their synagogue was torched, and Jewish-owned stores were destroyed. Herbert, 12, and his brother, 15, were left behind with their mother. Desperate to find a way out of Germany, she eventually found an uncle in London who agreed to sponsor them.

Although Herbert's mother was only entitled to one visa for her husband, the English consul, a "righteous Gentile," according to Herbert, stamped all four of them. Three weeks later, Herbert's father arrived on the family doorstep, 30 pounds lighter and haggard in appearance. The German soldiers had taken him to Buchenwald, a concentration camp, and only released him because in his wallet were papers revealing decorated (Honor Cross) military service. The family stayed up all night while Herbert's father recounted his harrowing experience.

Recognizing that as an adult male, he was particularly in peril, Herbert's father left for England the next day. Herbert's brother, having secured an apprenticeship, followed six weeks later. Herbert and his mother remained behind for six months, attempting to obtain additional visas for his grandparents. Although

they left a month before the war began, tragically they were not able to get Herbert's grandparents out in time.

Although the family was finally reunited in England, they had very little money to survive. Herbert's parents lived in a one-room apartment, and his brother lived with his employer. His parents decided to send Herbert, who was now 12, to a B'nai B'rith boarding school in Kent, England. Although this Orthodox school was different from what Herbert had known, he learned a great deal about Judaism and made many new friends. "It also taught me you can adjust," he recalls.

Eager to immigrate to America, Herbert's family's sponsor in the United States was able to find a farmer in Alabama willing to teach the Kohn family how to farm. A highly educated and cultured family, they knew nothing about farming, but they were willing to learn if it ensured their survival. They arrived in New York and were met by Joe Heyman, their sponsor's brother. A few days later, with 14 pieces of luggage, they boarded a bus bound for Birmingham, Alabama and arrived in the small nearby town of Demopolis. The farmer began teaching them how to farm and milk cows. Herbert would get up early every morning and daven, or say his morning prayers, until it was time for work. He earned an allowance of 25 cents a week. "It was enough for a movie, popcorn and an RC Cola," he recalls. The local Jews encouraged Herbert's family to speak English, saying, "You're not in Germany anymore." They worked on their employer's farm for a couple of years and eventually were able, with assistance from their sponsor, to rent and stock their own farm.

In Demopolis, there were about 3,000 blacks out of a total population of 5,000. "I had never seen an African American before," recalls Herbert. He saw a connection between how African Americans were treated and how the Jews had been persecuted in Germany. Under the laws of segregation, African Americans couldn't even walk the streets at night. "It seemed like they had just gotten out of slavery," he recalls. "Conditions for them seemed a lot like what we experienced in Germany."

Although he and his family were now secure in America, Herbert did not forget his fellow Jews in Europe and the war that was still raging. In 1945, at the age of 18, Herbert was drafted into the U.S. Army and volunteered for early induction. After basic training, he was sent to Germany to fight against his native country. He arrived in Germany two days before World War II ended. "All the people celebrated that the war was over. I was the one who didn't celebrate," he says. "I felt cheated. I was supposed to be the fighting infantry man. But I didn't get a chance to do my thing for my family. I'd lost my grandfather, other family members and lots of friends."

Although the war was over, he still had an important role to play. Because he spoke German, he became his commanding officer's interpreter. It took a week to travel 300 or 400 miles because Germany was so damaged. "Everything was in disarray," he remembers. Serving as an interpreter, he visited D.P. camps teeming with refugees and saw first-hand the fate his family had so luckily escaped. Herbert remained in the reserves for 26 years and eventually became a lieutenant colonel.

After returning to America, Herbert attended Auburn University and graduated with a degree in agriculture and animal husbandry. After marrying and having two children, Herbert decided he wanted to become an accountant. He received his CPA certificate. After working as an accountant for several years, at age 40, he became the chief financial officer for a building construction firm.

Herbert's first wife, Elaine, died after 38 years of marriage. He remarried a widow, Frances Goodman. Between them, they have 11 Jewish grandchildren. Herbert belongs to three Atlanta synagogues: Congregation Shearith Israel, Congregation Shaari Shamayim, and Congregation Beth Shalom of which he is a founding member, as well as Congregation Shearith Israel in Columbus, Georgia.

He has returned to Germany several times, once on a Jewish Federation mission and has worked with survivors, pursuing reparation payments from Germany. He found one visit quite moving. The city of Frankfurt in recent years has reached out to Jews like Herbert who had been persecuted or pushed into exile. They have invited them back, paying almost all their expenses and putting them up in a very expensive hotel. "We had a lot of misgivings about going at first," he explains. "But I was surprised how they wanted to heal their guilt. We were treated like 100% VIPs. It was unbelievable how we were treated, with respect."

Herbert spoke to high school students in Germany and was impressed with their education and maturity and how much they had been taught about the Holocaust. "I visited my family's gravesides, the home where I lived and the two schools I went to, the Jewish school and the school I was kicked out of." Herbert found his rusty German returning by the end of the two-week trip, and his wife, apprehensive at first, fell in love with the city.

"Some people back in Atlanta didn't want to hear this," he says. "But I wrote that the Germans were strongly interested in reconciliation, in healing the bad things they had done to the Jewish people. They knew more about the history than I ever thought. They had restored records, established museums, and they were very interested in recognizing that we were the victims of some of the bad deeds of their ancestors."

A German student asked why he had been ready to fight against the land of his ancestors, and Herbert told him why. But he also realized, he said, that he was no longer an 18-year-old willing to fight for vengeance. "I have tried to remove the word 'hatred' from my vocabulary, as well as 'retaliation' or 'revenge,' because I've learned in 60 some years that these words don't make things better. They don't heal any other problems." Other words may help, and so Herbert has made speaking about the Holocaust the mission of his retirement. He speaks at countless schools and universities.

He still thinks about the segregation he saw when he first came to America. He knows where it can lead. Recognizing that each of us must work actively to make conditions better for all, he agreed to help the City of Atlanta to form a non-profit organization helping to provide affordable housing for inner-city families. Herbert's words of advice to children: "All of us have a role to play to make a better world. Don't be bystanders."

nba draft choice 1963

Every great athlete can share a tale of hard work, perseverance, and endless practice. But Andre Kessler can also tell a story of secrecy, fear, and courage. One might wonder how Andre went from hiding from the Nazis in a library to sharing a hotel room with a fellow NBA player, the legendary Wilt Chamberlain.

Born Andrei Grunfeld in 1940, Andre grew up in Bucharest, Romania as an only child in a multi-ethnic upper-class neighborhood. His father was a businessman who owned a men's shirt factory, and his mother was a loving housewife. Together with Andre, they formed one of the only two Jewish families in his apartment building. Born with light hair and blue eyes like his mother, no one suspected that Andre was Jewish, nor did they care. That is until 1942, when the Nazis arrested his father.

Andre's life changed dramatically when he was only two years old. He and his mother were forced to hide in a small room in their apartment near their bathroom, aided by their building's superintendent, Glaourgi Popscu, who brought them food. "The room was very cramped," Andre recalls, especially for a little boy who wants to play. The only times Andre and his mother could leave the room

was when an air raid siren went off. They lived in this tiny room for two and a half years, until Andre was five. "To keep me quiet, my mother taught me how to read and write. By the time I was four, I was fluent in both Hungarian and Romanian," Andre recalls.

Andre's father returned in 1945 after the war ended, 114 pounds lighter than when he left. He had been forced to work at a slave labor camp at the border of Romania and the old Soviet Union. He described his life digging ditches at the camp as a "hell-hole." Fortunately, he had a life to return to. "When my father was forced to sell his shirt factory because he was Jewish, he sold it to his Gentile partner," Andre explains. "This kind man sold it back to my father in 1945."

When Andre was about 6, he began first grade at a Romanian public school. "I didn't know how to interact with other kids. I was in constant trouble for biting and hitting, but finally I adjusted," Andre says. Later, his mother decided that it was important for her son to know his Jewish roots, so she took him to a yeshiva to study Hebrew three times a week.

For a while, life resumed its normality. Andre continued school while his father worked in his factory all day. But in 1947, the Communists gained control of Romania. "My father's business was nationalized so that he could run it but no longer own it," explains Andre. But his parents were stubborn, and not about to let the Communists determine their future. They soon arranged for Andre and his mother to flee.

With the help of paid guides, Andre, now 8, and his mother traveled over two borders - from Romania to Hungary to Austria -

through gaps in the barbed wire. Eager to escape, Andre and his mother shared one bag that held a change of clothes and some pictures. Andre still remembers the patrol guards, the cigarette smoke, and the sound of barking dogs along the borders. His mother stepped into a pot hole and twisted her ankle. The minute they snuck into Budapest, they sought shelter in another safe house. Once again, young Andre was told to be very quiet. Once his mother's ankle healed, they crossed into Austria.

When they arrived, the Austrian police immediately arrested them and sent them on a bus to Vienna. "My father followed soon after, but before he left, he blew up his factory so the Communist government wouldn't have it," Andre recalls. "He also made sure to send funds to the Austrian bank so that we would have some money waiting for us."

Andre's father had two brothers living in France, so instead of going to Austria to join his wife and son, he decided to meet up with his siblings. When Andre's father arrived in France, he worked for the Citroen car company. "My mother and father divorced long distance," explains Andre. "Later we received word that my father met a Jewish French Holocaust survivor, and they married. I didn't see my dad for 13 years after that. But he always stayed in touch." In Austria, Andre's mother used her maiden name, Kessler, and Andre took it as well.

In March 1951, Andre's mother was cleared to travel to the United States. They boarded a ship that was divided into two sections: male and female. "For the first time in my life, I was separated from my mom," Andre recalls. He was 11 at the time and was excited about seeing America. On the ship, Andre experienced his first taste of freedom - unlimited food.

Mother and son arrived in New York on April 17, 1951. His mother's brother, Emory, had guaranteed their care, so they didn't need to enter through Ellis Island. Emory took them to the home of Andre's Uncle Alex in Queens. "Emory drove a big Cadillac, and although I spoke no English, I loved the feeling of driving down Broadway with the top down," Andre reminisces. "I remember the beautiful neon lights and the famous Camel sign. That was my first impression of America."

In Queens, he and his mother had to start a whole new life for themselves. "This is America. You get nothing for nothing," Andre declares. "My mother had never worked before. She got a job in a doll factory working from 3 to 11:00 p.m. She stapled clothes to dolls. Her hands swelled like a catcher's mitt." Later, Andre's mom took a job in a textile company where she worked for 34 years. "Although my mom spoke fluent English, she never lost her accent," Andre remembers.

Andre was placed in sixth grade at an American public school. He knew no English, and in those days there was no help available for foreign students. Luckily, Andre had an exceptional ear for language, and, within only 10 months, he had a working knowledge of English. After almost a year of school, Andre found himself hanging out with a gang. Truancy letters arrived in the mail, but Andre somehow convinced his mother that they were letters of commendation.

Although Andre was hanging out with a shady group of kids, which might suggest bad judgment, he did have one exceptional skill - sports. He inherited his ability from his father, who had formed a Jewish soccer team to compete against Romania's national team when Jews were barred from it. By the time Andre was in seventh grade, he was playing five sports: baseball, soccer, track, rifle team and basketball. Andre was often socially promoted to the next grade because his coaches needed him. But still, Andre continued his rebellious ways. He lived in a tough neighborhood and was often compelled to use his fists.

Just two weeks before Andre was scheduled to graduate high school, he stole a car. He was taken before a judge and given two choices: military school or jail. He chose military school and was immediately taken to a Naval recruiting station where he entered basic training. "When I was stationed as a medic in Washington D.C., I began playing basketball," Andre says. It wasn't long before a scout for New York University spotted him and arranged for his early release from the Navy. He started school as a sophomore at NYU in 1961 on a full scholarship. Andre and the rest of his teammates were expected to take challenging courses and do well, so he worked hard at school and remained eligible to compete in games.

In 1963, Andre was drafted by the Philadelphia Warriors and played for two years until his knees gave out. "Back then, the NBA was very different. It was still basically a white league," Andre explains. "The owner decided it would be interesting to have a black man and a Jew rooming together, so I was put into a room with Wilt Chamberlain." When Wilt wasn't allowed to stay in the same hotel as his white teammates, the whole team would stay in Wilt's hotel to show their support. Years later Andre, who had ordered Sports Illustrated for his son, was surprised to see himself on the magazine's cover in the background of a Chamberlain photo.

In 1965, Andre got a job with a textile company which sent him to Atlanta, Georgia. In the South, Andre went by the name of Andy. At age 30, Andy considered himself a "confirmed bachelor," but he met Marsha Tennebaum in 1973, and they married shortly after. He retired in 2002 as a manufacturing representative.

Andy and Marsha have a daughter Gena and a son Laurence. It was always important to Andy that his kids grow up in a Jewish environment. They were one of the founding families of Congregation Etz Chaim synagogue in Atlanta, and he currently attends services every Saturday at Congregation B'nai Torah.

"The good Lord and I have some interesting conversations, although I seem to do all the talking," muses Andy with a smile. He wears two things on his neck: a mezuzah, given to him by his aunt in 1948 right before she crossed into Hungary, and a chai, because of his great respect for life.

Currently, Andy lives in Marietta, Georgia and volunteers as a docent at the William Bremen Jewish Heritage Museum and Kennesaw State University's Anne Frank exhibit. He works to teach others about the terrors of the Holocaust. He was recently reappointed chairman of the Georgia Holocaust Commission's Advisory Committee. Andy finds this particular role gratifying. He calls it ironic that he was the kid the teachers always said, "When are we getting rid of him?" Now he is teaching educators. "Hashem [God] works in mysterious ways."

Andy urges children to remember that being a bystander is as bad as being a victim or a perpetrator. He reminds us that we can fight discrimination in daily life. Wilt Chamberlain's former roommate cites as an example racial comments, "Don't laugh at racial jokes, because they're not funny."

one of the lucky ones

Regine Rosenfelder was an ordinary little girl living in Antwerp, Belgium during the 1930s. She loved her dolls and was surrounded by family, including many cousins and her grandparents who lived upstairs. She had one sister, Suzy. Regine had what was, in her words, a "happy childhood with a wonderful father who was very patient." Her family was not very religious and only went to synagogue on holidays, but they observed Shabbat, and on Friday night, lit candles. Chanukah was always an anticipated event, with many presents. On weekends, they vacationed at the beach, in Middlekerke, a resort town, a close distance by train. "It was the best time of my life, being all together in one house with my cousins," she recalls. Regine attended a Jewish day school called Tachkimony. As a child she spoke Flemish, but she knew Yiddish so that she could understand her grandparents.

When the war started in 1940, "all of a sudden, everyone was focused on the radio. I could hear the sirens," Regine explains. "As a child you suddenly see your parents preoccupied with the news. I hated to see them huddled around the radio. It was very frightening. Everyone was going down in the basement in case the bombs were coming. This was the beginning of a lot of turmoil and fear." In May 1940, with news

of the Germans' advance upon Belgium, many Jews left Belgium, including Regine and her family. Regine remembers, "You could only bring so much. I took only the bare necessities in a small suitcase, and I had to leave all my dolls and toys." The train station was very crowded, and there was a great deal of commotion as people struggled to board the packed trains.

As the family prepared to leave, it was particularly traumatic to leave behind her beloved pet. Regine continues her story, "I had a little dog whose name was Molly. What were we going to do with her? I was very attached to her. We couldn't leave her in the house. When we left, she followed us to the station, and I kept hoping that she could come with us. The whole family was meeting up at the train station. It was a tremendous hall, and there are a million steps going up to the train platform. My little dog was still following us all along. We got to the train station and had to climb the steps to get to the platform. Just going up the steps with that heavy bundle made me think I would fall backwards. All of a sudden, Molly disappeared. That hurt. We went on without her."

Regine continues, "I don't think we even bought a ticket. We just pushed into the train. No one was checking tickets. Everyone tried to get out of Belgium. We were trying to get to France because France was still unoccupied. We didn't know where else to go. We got on the train to France and transferred a number of times. As we were advancing, you could see the fires where the bombs had hit. The cities were burning. The train would stop. We'd have to get out and hit the grass because of the bombs. We continued like that until we got to France. The time element is hard to remember. The days and nights get confused. Too many people were in the train. I remember my father bleeding from his nose. Everyone was trying to stop him from bleeding. The trains were open – not passenger trains. These were trains that ferry cargo. To this day, whenever I see those trains coming by, the memories come flooding back of that trip."

They arrived in Vicque, a little French town, in May 1940. The entire family stayed in one big house, except the grandparents, who lived in a little house across the street. The people in Vicque tried to make life comfortable for them and even let them live in the house for free. Even though the townspeople accepted them and made them feel like part of the community, Regine and her family had no close friends there. The children attended school, and for a while, everything was fine. However, this situation didn't last long since the French government began rounding up Jewish men. The men in Regine's family had to report to a French work camp called Camp Fremont.

In August 1940, Regine's Aunt Monie gave birth to Beatrice (Betty) in Ebreulle, a neighboring town where there was a hospital. Although the women and children remained, without the men to provide food, survival was difficult. "No one worked, and I don't know how we survived. We must have traded things for food," Regine surmises. A few weeks later Regine's entire family was sent to the same French work camp, but soon after, the French released the women, the children, and Regine's elderly grandfather. At that time, the remaining family members were not aware the men had been deported to Auschwitz, never to be seen again. "My father had a ring with his initials. Somebody brought the ring back to us [after he was sent to Auschwitz]. My mother kept it with her throughout

the war," Regine remembers.

After they were released from the work camp, Regine and her family returned to Vicque. Because Vicque was no longer safe, they moved to an abandoned train station in the country. In addition to an unending variety of creative "train" play available to the children, they also raised chickens and rabbits. Life grew easier as their vegetable garden blossomed to provide their own food. They remained in the country station for a year.

Because the family's safety was always in jeopardy, in 1941, the Jewish underground, Secure Des Enfants, placed Regine, her sister Suzy and three cousins in a children's home called Chateaux des Morelles. "There we were safe, but miserable. The food was horrendous, and the amount of children there made things considerably worse because there was no one to really take care of you. We ate a lot of mush. Instead of putting sugar in the mush one day, they put in salt. They gave it to all the kids, and the kids started to throw up. You had to eat it. The entire children's home was throwing up. They'd cook leeks in a white sauce. I couldn't swallow them, but would pass it on to the kid next to me ... We stayed there through the winter because I remember wearing my wooden shoes, my feet freezing. We had to go in the middle of the night to get milk from the farmer in metal vats, and my feet were freezing," Regine recalls.

While Regine, her sister and cousins lived at the children's home, Regine's mother Sally and her sister, Aunt Sabine, took care of a rich Jewish family at a resort in Chamberre. The Jewish family managed to get Regine, sister Suzy and cousin Lucy to the resort. Of all the times during the war, this was the best; it was heaven. Regine learned how to read French books and play the piano, but it didn't last more than three weeks, as everyone had to leave because of the impending danger. Living situations were always temporary because the Germans didn't stay put. As they advanced, the children often had to be moved overnight. Regine, Suzy and Lucy were uprooted again and came to live in another children's home called Au Savoir in the mountains. They stayed there throughout the cold, bitter winter of 1942. They had no heat, and blankets were scarce. The harsh winter caused many infections and boils.

The Jewish underground network, Secure Des Enfants once again was charged with moving the children to safety in 1943. From Au Savoir, they stayed at a convent with many other children in Grenoble, France. The nuns changed their names so that they wouldn't arouse suspicion. Regine Dollman became Renee Bollman; Suzy became Suzanne, and Lucy became Louise. Not longer after, Regine and her cousin Lucy moved to a private home with people paid to provide shelter to young Jewish children. They were put to work taking care of the women's babies and picking grapes. The grape picking was hard work, and in the cold, their hands rapidly cracked and bled. They had unbelievable lice and sores from poor hygiene, and again there was no one to take care of them.

Despite the harsh conditions, Regine never forgot the woman who gave birth to her. "I saved every little piece of paper from my mother – addresses where she had lived," Regine remembers. "They told us we'd have to bury the addresses or we'd be found out, and our families would be killed. I was getting desperate, so I took the last known address of my mother, wrote out a card and put our address on the back of it. I took a chance that she'd find us. All of a sudden I thought I was lost in this world and that my mother would never find me." Excitedly, Regine continues, "One day, close to 1945, my mother comes up the mountain . . . The card that I had sent was forwarded from one address to the next address until she received it."

"Children got lost like this all the time," Regine explains. "There were no records left. No one knew to whom these kids belonged. Kids were placed; parents were deported, and no one had a record of who was placed where. Our mother came and witnessed our poor condition. She couldn't take us then, but she got in touch with a group who could."

The only man in the family who survived the camps was Regine's cousin, Willy. Even though he lived, Auschwitz left him with typhoid fever. Willy got married in 1946, and his wife had a baby. Willy remained ill, and because medicine was scarce at the time, he died when the baby was 1 year old. Regine soon found out her father had not died in the gas chamber at Auschwitz but at Dachau after mistakenly eating a poisonous root. Cousins Lucy and Betty lost both their parents.

After the war, the family who survived returned to Belgium, and Aunt Sabine repossessed the house that she had before the war. Regine, her mother, her sister, her Aunt Frieda, and her grandfather moved in with Aunt Sabine.

Two years later, at age 16, Regine and her mother moved out. They needed money, so Regine's mom opened a store selling liquor and black-market cigarettes. Regine also worked to make ends meet. "In the evening,

I'd pick up wholesale pearls where my sister and I would put on the end piece to make it a necklace. It was piece work," Regine recalls.

At this time, Regine's Uncle Charles, her mother's brother, was living in Atlanta, Georgia and wanted to move the family to the United States. They obtained the necessary papers for Regine and her two young cousins, and in 1948, they immigrated to Atlanta and stayed with her aunt and uncle. Regine, Herbie and Freddie arrived in June, and during the summer they learned English, although they could not speak it very fluently. Regine attended Bass High School and went to the synagogue. She spent many days and nights socializing with other European teenagers as part of the "New World's Club." They'd play ping-pong or dance to the jukebox while adults served them refreshments. "That's how we dated and got together, and I met my husband at one of those 'New World's Club' gatherings," Regine fondly explains.

Regine was married on November 4, 1951 to John Rosenfelder at Congregation Beth Jacob in Atlanta. She has two children, Cindy and Henry. She was president of the congregation's sisterhood and later of Hadassah. Today she sits on the advisory board for Eternal Life Hemshech, an organization of Holocaust Survivors and Second and Future Generations. In addition to holding a variety of retail positions, Regine has worked at the Thomas Eye Group for the past 10 years. She is at an age to retire but keeps "putting it off." The two cousins who immigrated to the United States with her are practicing doctors, one of them in Atlanta. Regine's daughter lives across the street with two children, and her son lives nearby and is married with one daughter. Her mother is 99 years old and lives independently at the Zaban Jewish Tower in Atlanta. Her Aunt Sabine lived to be 106 years old and died in New York with daughter Lucy by her side.

All that Regine endured during the war, and her struggle after the war to continue on with her life, would not have been possible without her family. Even though she was surrounded by despair and neglect, she saved every postcard from her mother, so that she could remain hopeful and would someday see her mother again. Regine was one of the lucky ones; many had survived the war only to find their entire family had perished. Her message to American teenagers is to enjoy what they have because, she says, "It's really not that bad. Just think about it; it could be worse."

"To make a life and watch your children grow, that is what makes you happy."

mr. flag builds a city

"Money grows on trees here; you just have to bend down and pick it up," Ben Gross, who built an entire city in Georgia, declares about America.

Life wasn't always full of such opportunity for Ben. Born in 1921 in Palanok, Czechoslovakia, a poor military town, Ben was dealt a harsh hand of cards. He slept in a single bed with his five brothers and one sister under a leaky roof in a cramped home. Ben wasn't formally educated. Aside from one or two hours a day spent in Hebrew school, the balance of his education came from playing "heddar" – school – with his friends and siblings. This was the way of life for Ben's family, and they accepted it. His father was a tailor who worked hard to earn a living. His brothers were tailors, also. From the day he was born, Ben was expected to become a textile worker, in hopes that he would make enough money to help support the family. Ben was determined to forge a new path.

Hard times loomed for Czechoslovakia, cut up by Germany in 1939. Palanok was taken by Hungary which was controlled by Germany, and anti-Semitism raged. Ben, by now 18 years old, escaped it by fleeing alone to Budapest, Hungary around 1940. "You could get

lost easier than [in] a little town," he says.

Once in Budapest, young Ben lived alone in boarding houses and tried to make a living with menial jobs. One night, his dream of building a new life in Budapest was shattered by a knock on the door. The Hungarian Nazis were sending away all of the Jews in Budapest. Ben was taken to a labor camp in Romania. All Hungarian men were subject to the draft, but Jews weren't allowed to be soldiers and instead were forced to perform military labor. The Hungarians did, however, force them to march to work with their shovels as if they were guns. Ben, now a slave laborer, dug holes, cut trees and worked on the railroad wherever he was needed near the Hungarian-Romanian border. He was held for more than two years, with no hope of escape. The prisoners starved, and many of them died. Ben had worked with his uncle, a kosher butcher. They had secretly koshered meat for Jews in their area after it became illegal, and Ben used that experience to work in the camp's kitchen. He received additional food to eat and was able to maintain his weight more so than other captives.

In late 1944, near the war's end, Ben found an opportunity to escape. "The Germans were confused about what to do with us. They didn't have anywhere for us to go," Ben reminisces. One night, he and three other prisoners slipped away while on a march. They hid on a farm in a hole in the ground, and in a few days, the Russian army came through.

Just after he escaped, Ben spotted his brother Bernie, still a slave, being marched through the streets with another labor detachment. Ben and Bernie made eye contact, acknowledging each other's survival, but made sure not to show any recognition. Until then, he didn't know Bernie was still alive. Despite this hopeful moment, Ben's chances of seeing the rest of his family again seemed dim.

After liberation, he worked as a translator for the Russians. When Germany was defeated in 1945, desperate to get back to Czechoslovakia, Ben paid a woman to smuggle him over the border. He arrived in Prague and soon thereafter, things began to improve. He heard that refugee children were being sent back to Prague on trains. "I checked every day for my sister on the trains," he says softly, his voice catching. Finally, Ben found her. She was alive, but weighed only 70 pounds as a 12-year-old. Ben gathered up his sister and sped her to the hospital on the back of his motorcycle. For three weeks, Ben faithfully sat by his sister's side as she recuperated in the hospital. It was shortly after his sister's release from the hospital that Ben spotted his brother Bernie on the streets of Prague. Amazingly, all seven Gross family siblings were soon reunited. Tragically however, both parents had been killed in the Holocaust.

In 1945, Ben became an interpreter for the Jewish Joint Distribution Committee translating Czech into Hungarian, Yiddish and Russian. While working as an interpreter, Ben heard from his Uncle Eugene Lebowitz, his mother's brother, in the United States about a possible job opportunity there as a butcher. He knew he could only escape the chaos and poverty of Czechoslovakia by leaving the country. He dreamt of freedom and prosperity in America and knew he had to find a way to this land of opportunity. Luckily, Eugene, his two brothers and his sister were willing to sponsor Ben and his family. Things looked promising for them, but then reality set in. To bring seven people to America was difficult, and America still wasn't letting in refugees. It took several years, but finally in 1949, the American relatives sent for Ben and his many siblings.

It was miraculous that all seven of the siblings survived the Holocaust, and now they wanted to remain together, never to be separated by prejudice again. Ben, Bernie and Bill came first. Rosalyn soon joined the first three in America, and Alex arrived by December 1949. Sam came in 1954 after serving in the Israeli Army. It took the family 25 years to get Philip out of Palanok. He was stuck inside the Soviet Union, living in the family's old house.

Ben arrived in New York at Ellis Island, eager to forge a new life. From there, the brothers went to Ellwood City, Pennsylvania. Ben knew no English and couldn't even write his name. However, despite this language barrier, Ben quickly managed to lease a home and get a job with a butcher, working on Sundays for a kosher butcher to make extra money. Earning up to $100 a week, Ben thought he was rich. This routine of seven-day work weeks went on for nearly a year until Ben, eager for a new opportunity, moved to nearby Pittsburgh. There, industrious and independent, he started his own butcher business.

Within a few months, life dealt Ben a surprisingly pleasant card. Sylvia Smooke was a pretty American girl whose mother occasionally stopped by Ben's butcher shop with her family. He carried her packages to the car and struck up a conversation in Yiddish. Thinking she was attractive, he asked, "Do you have any daughters who look like you?" He met one of those daughters, Sylvia, not long after at his sister Rosalyn's wedding in August 1949. "Everything about her was special, from her looks on down," Ben says with a grin. Ben and Sylvia were engaged by Rosh Hashanah (Jewish New Year), and they were married on December 18, 1949. They'd put off the wedding while waiting for Alex to arrive in the United States so he could be the best man.

For the next 15 years, Ben worked hard at his butcher shop in Pittsburgh and then at a supermarket in Ellwood City, where he rose to the position of manager. Later, he joined his brothers, now in the prefab housing business in Youngstown, Ohio, and for six months lived there while Sylvia ran the business back in Pennsylvania. In 1963, following his brothers' suggestion, Ben and Sylvia decided to move to Atlanta to expand the housing business. Soon after they arrived, Ben spotted another new opportunity.

Ben heard of land for sale about 30 miles east of Atlanta. He and a friend, a fellow survivor named Abe Grabia, surveyed it. Although it was night, and he couldn't see the land very well, Ben took a wild chance and bought the property on the spot. He had no real estate experience and couldn't even sign his check in English, but Ben, whose childhood and home were destroyed in World War II, had a vision to build his own city.

It took more than five years for Ben and Abe to work out the structure of the city, which would eventually become Conyers, Georgia. Conyers began as one road with only four or five homes. Little by little, more land was purchased and developed. As the sewer systems, water, and electricity in Conyers began running, more homes were built and sold. After years of hard work, all the money and energy were finally starting to pay off. Ben especially enjoyed developing lakes in the city. "There are about 20 lakes there now," he says with a twinkle in his eye. "Today you can see Ben Gross Lake." Slowly, Ben rebuilt the life which war had so brutally destroyed.

Ultimately, Ben and his brothers bought and developed a total of 3,000 acres in Conyers. Ben shakes his head in amazement acknowledging, "I don't know north, south, east, or west. I can't read or write in English, but I managed to buy thousands of acres at pennies an acre. It's a city now!" Ben credits his success not to luck, but to hard work and his ability to spot an opportunity and exploit it.

Ben explains that with success comes the obligation to give back to one's community and profession. He was elected president of the Georgia Home Builders Association despite prejudice against Jews in 1962. "When I was running, the KKK was passing out signs not to elect me because I am Jewish. I guess [the voters] saw hard work instead,"

Ben says. He went on to serve many years as the group's president. He also developed many soccer fields in Conyers and created a vibrant youth soccer league there. While Ben never had the chance to play competitive youth soccer in Czechoslovakia, he feels "American kids deserve more, and I wanted to give something back." Ben's eyes tear up as he struggles to speak. "I love America. I owe this country."

An American flag attached to his garage ripples gracefully in the breeze, a sign of the deep love Ben has for his country. "America took me in even though I couldn't read, write, or speak the language." Ben is known as "Mr. Flag." He has given away thousands of flags and displays them all around his home. Ben has personally pinned flags on Presidents Reagan, Bush Sr., and Clinton at various civic events. There was even a flag flown at the US Capitol Building in his honor during the Reagan administration. "The greatest thing this country has is freedom and opportunity," he says of America.

But Ben is disappointed in the low level of patriotism in this country now. "American kids take freedom for granted. They [would] have to have it taken away to appreciate it." He shakes his head, remembering the little freedom he had as a child in Czechoslovakia. He admonishes Americans to appreciate their great country more. "They need to just wake up," Ben declares. From the man who took his destructed life and built it up again, Ben's message to future generations is to "look what I did. The opportunities are here but you have to keep looking and love this country."

eugen schoenfeld

watershed of my life

When Eugen first became a concentration camp inmate, he continued to fantasize of one day traveling the world; this is something he'd dreamed about before the war. He already knew several languages and studied French with a prisoner who worked next to him and spoke it fluently. But after some time, he began to lose his future goals. For him in the camp, "Neither the past nor the future existed for me; I just lived for the now." All he ever did was work, sleep, and eat if there was any food. "You reduced yourself to the lowest common denominator of life, just existence," he recalls.

Eugen Schoenfeld was born November 8, 1925 in the mostly Jewish town of Mukacevo in Czechoslovakia. Mukacevo had a big synagogue, and almost 17,000 of the town's people, two thirds of its population, were Jewish. Most were Hasidic or traditional Orthodox Jews. One of his grandfathers was Hasidic, the other traditionally Orthodox. His family was observant, and Eugen was tutored in the Talmud by a rabbi after school. "Judaism was a very big part of my life then, and it still is," Eugen explains. He attended a Hebrew language school his father and a number of other Zionist had founded that was a Jewish although secularly oriented school. His father, an ardent

Zionist, even brought Eugen to hear the Zionist leader Zev Jabotinsky speak in 1936. Eugen and his family lived in a small house that had a courtyard. One of three children, he shared a room with his younger sister, Ester and brother Benjamin.

In 1938, his hometown was occupied by Hungary, and anti-Jewish laws were quickly enacted, limiting how many Jews could own businesses, serve in the military or attend university. Eugen was able to finish "gymnasium," or high school, in 1943 at age 18. He had a good education. He already spoke German, Russian, Czech, Hungarian, Yiddish, Hebrew and even English, memorizing famous passages from Shakespeare.

Abruptly, in April 1944, all Jews in his region were rounded up and taken to Birkenau, the death camp of Auschwitz. Almost his entire family, including Ester, his little sister, and their brother Benjamin, died there. Only Eugen and his father survived.

Eugen finds it difficult now to express his feelings about his family's deaths. He experienced anger, but mostly sadness, he recalls. Now, he says, he tries not to dwell on his loss, but frequently he dreams that he has found them again. "Those memories still haunt me," he reveals.

Surviving selection at Birkenau, Eugen, his father and two uncles were sent to the Warsaw Ghetto as slave laborers to help clean up the rubble after the uprising of the previous year. The Germans wanted to clean the bricks, ship them to Germany and rebuild even as the Allies were bombing them.

At this time Eugen had two dreams. The first was, if he survived, to travel the whole world, and the second was to bike through Europe. Before his internment, he'd been fascinated by a book from his father's store about a man who had bicycled around Europe and North Africa. Faced with hard labor and despair, Eugen focused on these positive images as long as he could.

One day in August 1944, the Germans asked who among the prisoners needed transportation to Dachau, a concentration camp near Munich. "It was part of the German mentality of telling the big lie: 'Who is too weak to walk 100 kilometers? We'll give you a ride.'" His friend was about to step forward, but Eugen warned him against it. Sure enough, a few people who did step forward were shot.

Everyone then began a long march to Dachau. On the way, many simply dropped dead from dehydration and exhaustion. After walking a long time, they were forced to lay in a meadow to wait for trains. Upon boarding the cattle-car, Eugen found no water to drink. By the time they arrived at Dachau, only two-thirds of the marchers were alive.

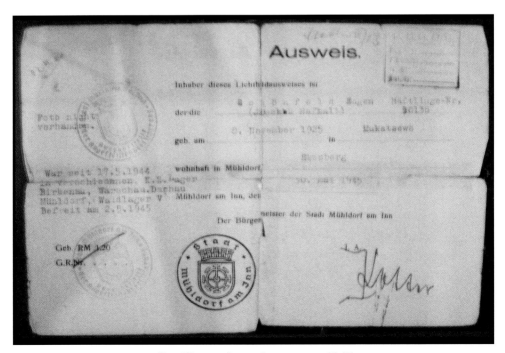

Certificate of statelessness — 1945

At the Muhldorf-Waldlager camp near Dachau, SS officers forced Eugen to carry 50-pound cement bags to the mixer. One time, he was carrying a bag up a steep incline and, hungry and weak, he began to waver. He was about to fall when an SS officer lifted the cement off of his back. The officer then brought Eugen over to his knapsack and gave him some of his own bread to eat. "Right then and there, I realized that we shouldn't judge people by the collective," Eugen explains.

Just before the Americans liberated the camp in May 1945, the SS brought Jews back to the trains, most likely to kill them. Eugen escaped by hiding in a hospital where one of his uncles, a doctor, worked. French fighter pilots destroyed the train, unaware that it was full of Jewish prisoners. Eugen, his uncle and his father didn't know the Germans planned to burn the hospital where they were hiding; fortunately, the Germans fled from the advancing Americans before they could set it afire.

Once freed, Eugen's father went back to Mukacevo, now in the Soviet Union, where his book and stationery store miraculously had not been looted – the only one of the formerly Jewish shops left alone – because his father was so well-regarded there. He married a Jewish woman who had lost her husband in the Holocaust.

Eugen, meanwhile, visited his hometown, but as it was occupied by the Russians, he settled in Prague, attending medical school there. Eventually, he fled to Germany when the Communists gained control of Prague. In Germany, he was offered a job by UNRRA, the United Nations Relief and Rehabilitation Administation, as a social worker in a DP camp, and kept getting promoted to more responsible positions, ultimately directing a camp, at age 23. Wearing the UN's military uniform, he was the equivalent of a full colonel. "I had a high rank for a young whippersnapper," Eugen explains with a grin.

In 1946, Eugen earned a scholarship to Columbia University, but he was unable to receive a visa to travel to the U.S. until 1948. Ultimately, he decided to attend Washington University because he had an uncle in St. Louis. He earned his BA and MA in sociology there and his doctorate at Southern Illinois University. While in St. Louis, he met his wife, Jean, at Washington University's Hillel Foundation. Married for 54 years, Eugen and Jean have four daughters who all live nearby in Atlanta. They also enjoy six grandsons.

Because Eugen was separated from his father so long ago, he never expected to see him again, especially since his father was trapped behind the Iron Curtain. However, Eugen did see him one more time in 1967, when the Soviets gave his father permission to travel with his wife to Memphis, Tennessee, where Eugen was a sociology professor at Memphis State University. He did not remain in the United States, remembers Eugen, because his wife still had family back in Mukacevo. His father died of a heart attack in Russia in 1976, just before immigrating to Israel.

Eugen moved to Atlanta in 1970 to become the Sociology Department Chairman at Georgia State University. "I found myself in my domain, in my world, the place that I felt happy, comfortable," Eugen emphasizes. In 1995 he retired from GSU but continued lecturing at Georgia Tech University, also in Atlanta. Eugen, who had once studied Talmud every afternoon with a rabbi, specialized in the sociology of religion.

Slowly, his dreams returned, and, eventually, Eugen was able to fulfill them. In retirement, he was hired by Georgia Tech University for its Studies Abroad program. He has lectured on his specialty, including the Holocaust, in some distant and exotic places: Australia, New Zealand, Tahiti, the Cook Islands, Hong Kong, Singapore, Oxford. The list goes on and on. Now, he says, he's too old to travel that much.

The Holocaust certainly marked him, he admits. When he lost his dreams of the future while slaving in the rubble of the Warsaw Ghetto, "that had to be reestablished in me, even after I was freed. I try to tell people, the Holocaust was not like a Hollywood story, where at the end, the crisis is over and you live happily every after. When you were liberated, this was not the end of the Holocaust. Each of us carried with us the consequence of the Holocaust, and I still do. It was the watershed of my life. It marked my intellectual concerns later in life. In fact, I became a sociologist due to two influences: my father's ideals and teaching and the Holocaust."

beating the odds

At age 12, Tom Reed was known as Thomas Weissbluth and stood in line in front of the barracks at Auschwitz. Though he was only a boy, he had told everyone that he was 17, old enough to work. He was surrounded by a variety of people – rich, poor, wise and simple. But that didn't make much of a difference. All were wearing the same prison uniform, regardless of whom or what they had been in the past.

Tom heard a catchy tune, and he turned to see a young man whistling as he took out the trash. He leaned toward his father, Eugene, and asked what the strange melody was. "That is Hatikvah," replied his father. "It means 'hope.' When the state of Israel comes about, that will be the national anthem." Tom never forgot the moving tune, and he never forgot that for the Jewish people, even at the worst moment in Jewish history, there would always be hope.

Born in Miskolc, Hungary on October 2, 1931, Tom was raised in nearby Mezocsat. He spent his childhood playing games, reading, and going to the Jewish school where his father was principal. There was a strong Orthodox Jewish community in the town, and there were constant debates between the younger and older generations about Zionism. He had "a heck of a lot of fun" in his hometown, but that was

before deportation in 1944.

Even now, Tom can still recall his grandfather's parting words to his father as they left the cattle cars and were separated at the gates of Auschwitz. "You shall live a long life. I bless you and your descendents to survive whatever comes." Tom listened to the blessing, and he did survive, but only after enduring years of pain. In Auschwitz, Tom witnessed unspeakable horrors and cruelty, not only from the Germans, but also among the prisoners themselves. "A lot of people became animals, but most of the deeply religious people kept their humanity." He remembers talking to some children in the camp who "had it pretty good," only to learn that they were twins who Dr. Mengele performed medical experiments on and later killed.

He and his father were transferred after three weeks, first to a camp near Dachau, and then to a new slave labor camp at Muhldorf where the Germans were trying to build a jet fighter in an underground factory. Tom worked cleaning streets and doing carpentry. He came down with typhoid fever, and received no medical care but survived. For a time, he helped the Jewish doctor in the camp treat other patients.

In the spring of 1945, an S.S. man named Greif knew the end of the war was coming. He made a deal with Tom's father that he would do his best to save the two of them if they tried to save him after the war. Tom's father agreed, and when they were going to be transported, Greif convinced the other S.S. men to allow Tom and his father to travel with him in the boxcar hauling bread instead of being locked up with the other prisoners in cattle cars.

At one point, knowing the end was near, the Germans opened the cattle car doors telling the hungry captives they were free because the Americans had arrived. The Germans lied and began shooting anyone they found outside the cattle cars. Tom relates a horrific act that he witnessed first hand. "Sauer, an 18-year-old German soldier would take a puff from his cigarette, shoot a woman, take a puff, shoot another woman. Greif saved me from death then."

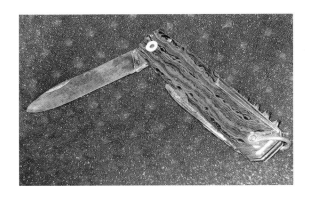

Tom was wounded when an American airplane shot up the German's train. Knowing they could no longer help each other, Greif changed into civilian clothes, gave Tom his wallet and knife, and fled. When asked if he was surprised that an S.S. man would save him, Tom shrugs, "There is human diversity. They had people of all kinds. I never saw Greif do anything bad." Tom never saw him again, but today, still has Greif's wallet and knife, mementos of his own liberation.

Five miles away, there was an elite Hitler youth school set up as a displaced person's hospital and camp. Two German doctors carried Tom from the train to the school. He refused treatment for his wound as he distrusted German doctors. At this lovely Alpine retreat that had been used for training Hitler Youth, Tom's father began a school for Jewish children, survivors of the Holocaust. General Eisenhower, who later became president, visited one day. So did the famous New York City mayor, Fiorello LaGuardia. He left his hat there, and Tom's father wore it for many years afterward.

In 1949, Tom moved to America with his father, the only other member of his family to survive the war. They went to Cleveland where they had distant relatives. Tom's father, an educated man, had to work in a factory. As a child, Tom had always loved reading, and he pursued his education here in the United States. He seized the opportunities that America had to offer and learned as much as he could. During Tom's junior year of college in Cleveland, he was drafted into the army for the Korean War. The time Tom served in the American army taught him discipline. He was put into intelligence because of the foreign languages he spoke. Tom recalls his military experience as another opportunity to educate himself. After the army, Tom continued with his education, graduating with an engineering degree later switching to international operations. He married his wife Lora on Labor Day 1955, and three children soon followed.

Tom's Cleveland relatives encouraged him to start his new life with a new American name. He randomly opened a phone book and saw the name "Reed." "I saw it and liked it," he recalls with a smile. "It was a short name." So from then on, Thomas Weissbluth was known as Thomas Reed.

Tom became an engineer and went to work for North American Aviation, a big defense firm that made airplanes in Columbus, Ohio, which later became part of Rockwell International. In Ohio, he also completed law school at night. He stuck with the engineering, though, and worked at the defense firm for 42 years. He worked building missile systems, contacting foreign businesses and government agencies, and later, using both his law and engineering degrees, was appointed by the Carter administration to an advisory committee dealing with the export of defense technology. Boeing eventually purchased Rockwell International and moved Tom's family to the Atlanta area. He retired five years ago, and his wife Lora, who taught school, retired with him.

While Tom certainly recovered from his Holocaust experience, he definitely did not forget it. A few years ago, Tom returned to Hungary for the first time since the war. Visiting his old, run-down synagogue, he stood in the deserted space and was hit with the realization that the people of his childhood were all truly gone. "In my mind, I could hear so clearly the prayers chanted within those walls by my family, friends and neighbors. I wondered, as I had so many times, how God had allowed this to happen." Of the 407 Jewish citizens who once lived in Mezocsat, only one Jewish person remains.

Today, you can find Tom teaching a Holocaust course for a continuing education organization, Seniors for Enriched Living. Or perhaps you will find him sitting in his favorite chair, reading a book from his private collection of over 2,000 books. Or maybe you will find him in the basement of his suburban Atlanta home, painting a canvas and using modern CDs as pallets. Or he might be creating a stained glass piece with his wife Lora. One thing, however, is certain. No matter where you find him, Tom no longer resembles the frightened child at Auschwitz that he once was. He is a man who has beaten all odds to live a successful life rich with learning and joy.

sad luck

"I had a diamond ring - a diamond engagement ring - and I wore it. The Germans took all of the gold, so I hid this ring. When I saw that they were searching the women, I said that they were not going to get that from me, so I swallowed it."

Nora Lewin didn't know if she'd ever see her husband again. Now, with everything else stripped from her – family, possessions, and dignity – she wanted to hang on to the one last possession that had any meaning to her.

She was born Nora Levin right after World War I ended in 1918 and spent her early years in Shavel, Lithuania. Lithuania was a modern country, growing fast, she remembers, and almost half her city's population was Jewish. Her family enjoyed going to the seashore or the countryside for the whole summer. They kept kosher, and they went to synagogue on holidays. She was close to both of her parents. She remembers her mother, Masha, who owned a fashion salon and made clothes, as very independent and smart, and her father, Michael, an accountant, as a very gentle and very good man. Nora was well-educated, having completed both a Hebrew and business school. She graduated from high school in 1938 and worked in a bank. She met her

future husband Joel Levin, who coincidentally had the same last name, and they married in July 1940.

When the war broke out, Nora was pregnant and visiting her parents in Shavel, but all communication was cut between it and Kovno, where she and Joel lived. And so, she and her husband were separated. Nora and her parents had already been herded into the Shavel ghetto when she gave birth to a son, Gideon, on November 27, 1941.

"He was my mother's joy," Nora declares. "If nothing else that I'm thankful for, it's that with all her sorrows, my mother had a pleasure of being a grandmother and seeing her first grandchild." Nora's mother used to bring milk for the baby, heating the bottle with her body's warmth. She, her mother and baby lived in a room with three other people. Her father and uncle had already been captured by the Germans – among the first to go because the Germans went after professional people first to make sure there were no leaders left.

Food was hard to come by. They were only given a quarter pound of bread a day and no meat at all. Extra food, for which people traded their own clothes or jewelry, had to be smuggled in. "All we owned was a bed, and in that bed I slept with mother and the baby. And the rats were all over; they were crawling on us," Nora recalls with a shudder. Jewish women were forbidden to bear children in the ghetto. Nora was only allowed to give birth to hers because the doctor at the city hospital was a friend from before the war and allowed Nora's mother to bring her there for delivery. At the Jewish hospital in the ghetto, Nora remembers, "The doctors used to hide that the babies were born." They had a secret brit (circumcision) for eight-day-old baby Gideon, supervised by a rabbi and a mohel, in the ghetto.

Meanwhile, Joel, a talented automobile mechanic for the Germans and protected by his supervisor for his handy work, was arrested in one attempt to get to Shavel to see his family in February 1942. That summer, though, he succeeded in getting German permission for his wife, son and her mother to join him and his family in Kovno. And finally he saw his son.

In Kovno, Nora says, "[Jewish] people were hungry; people were begging; they were coming to the houses and asking for a piece of bread. It was tragic." But Joel was managing to feed his family, and things were not so bad for them. They were together for a year and a half.

But in October 1943, the Germans separated them again. There had been rumors they would be taken to labor camps, but that families would be allowed to stay together. People simply didn't believe rumors that the Jews were being gassed to death and burned in crematoriums. Nora begged her mother, who wasn't on the list, to stay in Kovno, where she had a good job. But Nora's mother refused to leave them and insisted on coming along.

"In 1942, we were awakened by the Jewish police and taken in buses to be transported where they separated us," Nora explains. At the rail depot, children clung to their mothers' arms. Nora watched as the Nazis tore families apart, one by one snatching a member of a family and shoving them onto a different bus from the next person. As they got off the bus, the Germans separated the family. "My husband was on one side. I was holding my child, and he was taken away. My mother grabbed him and Gideon was taken from her," Nora painfully recalls. When Nora ran to them, a Nazi soldier hit her over her head with a gun. "They took my baby, my mother, and Joel's dad away from us. We never saw them again. We were put in freight cars and shipped like sheep."

Nora woke up on the freight train with dozens of other young women. Some cried; others silently awaited their fate. "When the train stopped, we were told we were in Estonia. Rumors were flying about the whereabouts of our husbands and children. The main rumor was that they were taken to Auschwitz where they were gassed and put in crematoriums," Nora sadly recalls.

Nora had left everything on the ground at the depot – all except her diamond ring. All her other jewelry was already gone, including her wedding band, which the Germans had taken. But about the engagement ring, her mother said, "Don't give that; let's hide it. You have something. You'll survive. One day, you'll have something from the past." And at the concentration camp, when she witnessed the guards searching all the women, making them undress, "I said no, they're not going to get it from me." And she swallowed it. She found it a couple of weeks later, in the camp, after she went to the toilet in the woods.

In Estonia, Nora first worked at a labor camp in Ereda. They worked in the snow, and some women died while marching miles to and from the camp. Later, at the Goldfieltz camp, she received a better job working indoors as a cleaning lady. To her great surprise, after a year, she learned through the Jewish underground, B'recha that her husband Joel was in a camp not far away. "One morning I looked up, and there Joel stood. He brought me good food and said to me, 'You look good.' " He told her he'd bring her to his camp. She became sick with typhoid fever and was about to be shipped to Auschwitz, when Joel came with a guard in a truck to pick her up. She went with him to the Kivioli camp, where the food was more substantial and the prisoners treated better. There she was hospitalized. Joel would stand outside the window – she was in isolation – and wave at her.

The Russians advanced on Estonia in 1944 and selections for Auschwitz began again. The sick and the children were taken first. One day a Russian bomb fell on the hospital where Nora was on the ground floor, and everyone thought she was killed. But she called out, and they pulled her from the wreckage. A German doctor told her, "You are a lucky woman. You will be in America one day." Nora explains, "I'll never forget that. I realized I was lucky. But it was a sad lucky. I lost my child, my mom, my dad, my siblings. It wasn't a real happiness. "

A few months later, in 1944, with the Russians approaching Estonia, Nora and Joel were separated yet again. They rode on the same train to Danzig and by boat to the nearby camp of Stutthof, where they were forced to part. She encountered unimaginable horror. "We saw the chimney where they were burning the people, the smoke that drifted up to the sky, day and night, night and day. Beatings, killings, abuses," Nora recalls. There were selections every day. There were only young women now. All the older ones had been killed.

From Stutthof, Nora was taken to Bromberg, a nearby labor camp, where she worked on the railroad in a big city, and where her Polish foreman, she remembers with gratitude, "was very kind to me. He used to bring me a cigarette once in awhile. When he used to go home for Christmas, he used to bring me back something to eat."

Nevertheless, camp life was so hard Nora was ready to give up. One day, after long hours of loading coal on trucks, when the inmates were black with coal, she was ready to refuse to do it anymore, come what may. But the other girls encouraged her to keep going. "You shouldn't talk like that. You were always encouraging us, saying that we'll survive. If you give up, everyone will give up."

In January 1945, nearing the war's end, the Nazis wanted to "drive the Jews into the sea." Marching with hundreds of other women, she decided to escape, and with about 10 other women, ran away. They found a deserted farm, where the Polish farmers had fled from the approaching Russians, and hid in a basement for three days. They found potatoes and a cow, which gave them milk. When the Russians came, the young women's liberation wasn't happy. The soldiers raped some of the women and shot one who resisted. "Somehow I was lucky because I was the only one who could speak Russian," Nora explains. A Russian officer urged them to leave for a big city, far away from the dangerous Russian soldiers.

With their heads still shaved and wearing their concentration camp rags, they were brought to Lodz, where Nora heard that her brother, her sister and her sister's family were alive. Another survivor, who got her old apartment back, gave Nora a room, a clean towel and clothes. "That's when I felt I was truly free," Nora declares. After a year, Nora moved to Vilna, Lithuania where she worked as a typist in a factory. One day someone came from Germany with a letter from Joel, who had not only saved her life, but those of others. In 1946, they were reunited in Munich.

"He met me at the train," she says. "He looked good. He had a good job with the Hebrew Immigrant Aid Society, HIAS; he was in charge of transportation. He dressed well and had a nice room in Munich." Nora got a job at HIAS too, registering people who wanted to go to the United States. Soon "we began thinking about moving on. I had relatives in the US, so did Joel." In 1946, Nora and Joel registered to immigrate to the United States of America.

Less than a year later, their immigration papers were approved, and on June 7, 1947, Nora and Joel arrived in New York after a seven-day journey by ship. Joel's cousins from Newberry, New York sponsored them. Nora and Joel changed their name from "Levin" to "Lewin." Nora went to school to learn English and was fluent within six months. She could now speak six languages – German, Russian, Hebrew, Yiddish, Lithuanian, and English. "Everyone came to see us; we were like miracle people," she fondly recalls. The Lewins lived in New York until 1985. They had two sons, Michael and Henry. Joel owned a used car business, and Nora was a homemaker. She took leadership positions in Hadassah and in her synagogue. The Lewins moved to Boca Raton, Florida in 1986, and fourteen years later Joel died.

Nora never told her children, until they were older, about her Holocaust experience. "It's a little hard for [young] people to understand. In the first place, I have a harsh accent. And they can't visualize what I went through. I am 85 years old, and I remember what happened to me when I was 23. I wish I had happier [memories.]"

She and Joel traveled to Germany twice over the years and testified in war crime trials. She identified one defendant – the doctor who had told her she was lucky - and Joel, who testified in German, recognized several. All of the defendants were sentenced to prison.

And that diamond ring? She managed to keep it for a little while in the camp, but, sure she'd lose it, gave it to Joel when he found her in Estonia. Joel, though, lost it to the Germans, who were constantly searching the prisoners. "It's not that important, but I wanted to show you, to tell you how, in all the bad times, people still tried to save some material things, as a memory, a sentimental thing." Even in the boxcar, she remembers, "every time the train used to stop we used to sing, because we never knew."

i owe my life to the italians

In the fall of 1938, 16-year-old Ed Berger, then known as Srecko Berger, was expelled from high school for playing pool with a few friends in an off-limits restaurant. Rather than wait a year to reapply, Ed opted to leave his hometown of Osijek, Yugoslavia and move to Zagreb, Croatia, where his aunt and her family lived. Though at the time it was most likely a disappointment for Ed, getting kicked out of high school was probably the best thing that could have happened to him. Had Ed stayed in Osijek, he would doubtlessly have been killed by the Germans along with so many of his family members who remained in Yugoslavia.

Born on November 13, 1922, Ed lived with his parents in Osijek until they divorced when he was 7 or 8 years old. He then lived with his grandmother until her death when he was 14. Ed was taken in by an uncle for two years until he moved to Zagreb. His family, like many Croatian Jews, was not very observant, but he did have a bar mitzvah.

Ed remained in Zagreb for three years, where he was very poor and received help from the Jewish community. He befriended a refugee from Vienna, Robert Abraham. Ed had taught himself to play guitar and would often play jazz guitar with Robert, a gifted pianist who

played with an American-style swing band called the Devil's Orchestra.

In April 1941, the Nazis occupied Zagreb. The schools were closed, so all the high school seniors were given their diplomas two months early. Naturally, all the graduates threw a party to celebrate their achievement. However, the party was at night and a curfew had been placed on the Jews. So Ed and a few of his Jewish friends simply took off their yellow star badges and went to the party anyway. It was a risk, but luckily none of the other graduates seemed to mind.

Ed's friend, Robert was called by the Germans to report to a "labor detail." Ed thought he would go with his friend, but his name wasn't on the list. The Germans really wanted ransom money from families for the boys'safety, but Ed didn't have parents to get money from. Robert Abraham never came back.

In July 1941, Ed slipped out of Croatia on a train. He knew that things would only get worse under the German occupation, and another friend's sister gave him an alias by which to travel. Because Zagreb was further west, Ed had a better chance to escape from there than he would have had in Osijek. Once on the train, Ed was noticed by his homeroom teacher, who also happened to be on the train. Instead of turning Ed in, his teacher gave him the name of a contact who would fix Ed up with the proper travel documents.

Over the next few months, Ed traveled back and forth between Ljubljana, Slovenia and Susak, Croatia. Sometimes he was with his uncle, Ernest Breder, who had also escaped from Zagreb. In Slovenia conditions weren't yet too bad for the Jews, but the Germans were only a few miles away. Susak was occupied by the Italians, but the Croatians there were very anti-Semitic.

In Slovenia, Ed lived for a while on a farm, where he pretended he was a Serbian Orthodox Christian. He and his uncle Ernest were nearly arrested more than once.

With his savings running out and the Croatian and Italian police looking for him, Ed decided to go to an Italian concentration camp in February 1942. While it may sound strange that someone would voluntarily go to a concentration camp, he had heard from the Ljubljana Jewish community that the Italians were humane and treated the Jews well. "I listened to the elders and the Jewish community," he says. "They had information, which I didn't, and I believed them."

Ed knew that if the Germans advanced, he would most likely be under much worse conditions than if he were under Italian control. And he was right. He doesn't know what happened to his father, but he was probably killed by the Germans in Belgrade, the capital of Yugoslovia. His mother and grandfather were killed by the Croatians at the Jasenovac concentration camp, as were most of the rest of Ed's relatives.

Ed and his uncle were sent on a train to the camp Ferramonte di Tarsia in Italy's distant south, far away from the Germans. However, Ed got off the train in Rome because he wanted to explore the city, which he had only seen in photographs. He was caught by the Italian police a few days later and told to get back on the train. Ed was quite adventurous and didn't

mind taking risks such as getting off the train. Years later, he looks back on his experience and says simply, "I was young and stupid."

When Ed arrived at Ferramonte di Tarsia, he was put in a barrack for unmarried men. He was not required to perform forced labor, but was often very hungry in the camp. They usually didn't have much to eat except garbanzo beans. Ed studied every day in the camp, mainly because he had always enjoyed learning and had nothing else to do. Ed met his future wife, Sultana Salomon, when she and her family, who had escaped from Belgrade, came to the camp in the spring of 1943.

Hitler kept pressuring his ally, the Italian fascist dictator Benito Mussolini, to deport Jews from Italy to Auschwitz. Mussolini's army and government didn't want to comply, and kept finding excuses to put off the deportations.

The Allies took control of Sicily in the summer of 1943 and then invaded Italy. By September 1943, Ed's camp was liberated. Sultana's father Moshe decided the family would be safest in Sicily because the Germans were unlikely to retake it from the Allies. Ed traveled with the Salomons to Palermo, where he studied chemistry at a university from 1943 to 1946. They then moved to Rome, and Ed married Sultana in 1947.

After earning his college degree in 1948, Ed and Sultana moved to Buffalo, New York, where Ed worked as a chemist. He and Sultana had two children, Ruth and Daniel. After Sultana died in 1969, Ed remarried. He and his wife Beni have between them four children, including Beni's children Steven and Debra, and nine grandchildren.

Now 81, Ed is still active and works as a translator. He knows Italian, German, French, and Serbo-Croatian. He credits his family for his love of languages, saying, "My family felt that unless you knew languages, you were not a complete person." The American Translators Association now gives an annual prize in his honor.

Ed feels he was extremely lucky to end up under Italian control. "I made the right decisions without knowing it, only in retrospect." It is because of the kindness shown by the Italians that Ed managed to survive and live a successful life. "I owe my life to the Italians."

equilibrium is the motto of my life

It was March 1946 in Salzburg, Austria. Harold Bowman gave Penina Weisz three yards of silk parachute fabric and a Star of David necklace. Harold told his fiancée that someday her wedding dress would be made from that very silk. He then left her behind, hoping that they would reunite in Palestine.

Harold was an American soldier whom Penina, a Holocaust survivor, had met while she was living in a displaced person's (DP) camp for young Jews in Salzburg. Harold was guarding German prisoners nearby and, asking to meet young Jews, was directed to the camp where Penina and her sister Miriam stayed. Harold taught Penina Hebrew so that they would have a language to share. Meanwhile, Penina's friend interpreted for them. Penina kept a notebook about what Harold taught her. In three months, the two were able to communicate.

Harold was sent back to the United States; it was time to part. He gave her the silk for which he'd traded cigarettes. Penina wrote to him in America, but her letters didn't have a return address, so Harold couldn't write her back. When he didn't respond, Penina feared the relationship was over. Desperate, she and her friends scraped together

some money for a telegram, and it was only from this telegram that Harold learned that she lived in a different camp. She and her group of 40 young survivors had moved from Salzburg to Brivio, Italy. Their correspondence resumed, and soon they each had a thick stack of letters.

Penina and the other girls from the camp were eager to immigrate to Palestine, but the British would not allow in new immigrants. One night Penina, her sister Miriam, and the group were taken aboard a ship that was to smuggle them into Palestine. Although she was told to leave behind any personal belongings, Penina sewed the precious fabric that Harold had given her into her coat lining. The ship they sailed on was intended to hold 80 fishermen but was carrying 800 survivors. The British caught the illegal ship, however, and they were transported to Cyprus to yet another detention camp. Two months later, Penina was finally allowed to enter Palestine.

Meanwhile, Harold had made his own way to Palestine and was studying engineering at the Technion University in Haifa. Ironically, it still took a while for them to find each other. Harold wrote to the British rabbinate for help in locating Penina. They told him she was in Cyprus. Harold passed a letter on to a British correspondent going there to let Penina know he was already in Palestine. In Cyprus, the British were only letting a few people a month out of the camp to go to Palestine. The group had to decide who should go first. They chose a pregnant woman, her husband and Penina, because Harold was waiting for her, as the first to enter.

When Penina arrived in Palestine, she was detained in yet another camp. While on a bus to the camp, she slipped a note out the window to a young girl in the street and asked her to get it to Harold Bowman at the Technion. The girl gave it to a professor who found Harold.

In May 1947, 18 months to the day after they met, Harold and Penina were married at a kibbutz near Haifa where she and her sister then lived. Her wedding dress was made from the silk parachute fabric that Harold gave her in Salzburg.

Penina's story truly began many years before. She was born in Cluj, Romania in 1927. She had two sisters, Yaffa and Miriam, and one brother, Mordecai. Penina was raised as a religious Jew. There were 20,000 Jews living in her town. There were synagogues, rabbis, Jewish schools, and a mikvah (ritual bath) which her parents owned. Growing up Orthodox meant Penina wore long-sleeved shirts, attended Jewish schools, and refrained from dating. "It was a 'Fiddler on the Roof' life. I'm glad I was brought up religious . . . I like the religious feeling," she explains.

In April 1944 Hungarian soldiers came to Penina's home and told her family that they had to prepare to leave for a work camp. Not knowing what really lay in store for them, they went. They were sent to Auschwitz where they were separated. Her mother was killed immediately. Her father and brother were sent to Dachau where her father died of typhus a week before liberation. Her brother survived the camp. Penina and her sisters stayed together at Auschwitz where they worked at hard labor, breaking rocks. They were there for six months.

At Auschwitz the prisoners had to endure repeated "selections."

Wanting to avoid selection, the sisters would linger near the line's end. They also noticed that the weak were typically selected first, so they often mustered a show of strength for the guards. Regardless, a few times she or one of her sisters was selected; however, they always managed to mingle back in the crowd that remained behind.

One day, the block overseer who guarded the barracks told the three Weisz sisters that today they should not avoid selection, as it would be a good one. She liked them, Penina said, because they worked hard and kept their place clean. They decided to trust her and were chosen in October 1944 to go to a labor camp, Mahrisch-Weisswasser, where they worked soldering wires in an electronics factory until the war was over in May 1945. Penina says that she woke up one morning in the camp; there was no gong; the soldiers were gone, and the war had ended.

Eager to return to her hometown Cluj, the Weisz sisters began an arduous journey on many different trains and even by horse-drawn buggy. When they finally arrived, they learned there was nothing left for them. She recalls her neighbors' cruel reception. "You back? We thought the Germans killed all of you." Penina remembers, "We felt like we didn't belong there."

Since Penina and her sisters saw no point in staying, they joined a youth group heading to Palestine. Penina's older sister, Yaffa, could not leave right away because she wanted to wait for her boyfriend. He arrived two weeks later, and they stayed in Romania until 1958 when they fled the communist country for Israel.

Miriam and Penina were sent to various DP camps: Budapest, Hungary, Bucharest, Romania, Graz, Linz, and Salzburg, Austria. The Jewish Joint Distribution Committee, known as "the Joint," helped them along the way. "They supplied me with my three Bs," Penina recalls. "Blankets, bread and bribes." They used this money to buy their way out of communist Hungary and to cross other borders on their way to Palestine.

Although united and married in Palestine, Harold and Penina did not live there long. In October 1947, Harold and Penina left for the United States. Penina remembers being amazed by the Empire State Building when they arrived in New York, and that she tried counting its many stories. She recollects, "Everything was clean and free, and no one could stop me. I could walk in freedom." They settled in Harold's hometown, Chicago, where his relatives welcomed Penina. Harold finished college at the University of Chicago and then went on to its law school. Penina worked as a secretary for her father-in-law. Penina remembers admiring her mother-in-law's bath robe, so on Penina's birthday her mother-in-law gave her the robe to keep. They also threw her first birthday party. In time, Penina assimilated into American culture, wearing lipstick and nylons and learning English, her seventh language.

Until Harold completed law school, the couple lived in the university's army barracks where Leora was born. Two more children, Allan and Deborah, followed. Eventually, the family retired to Atlanta. Penina and Harold now have three grandchildren.

Today Penina is active in her synagogue, Congregation Etz Chaim, and enjoys playing Mah Jongg. "I keep busy with hobbies," she explains. "I like to give and never receive." She knits, sews, needlepoints, and makes purses. She loves to garden and entertain and has taken courses in everything from ceramics to Chinese cooking.

She has learned not to get upset with little things. After the suffering she has endured, she realizes that material objects can always be replaced. Penina appreciates freedom, always votes, and never passes up an opportunity to voice her opinion. She has joined many organizations and often serves on their boards.

Reflecting on how her Holocaust experience has affected her life, she shares her philosophy. When she was learning English, Penina looked up the word "equilibrium" in the dictionary and became fascinated by it. One of its meanings is "mental balance." "I was determined to make the meaning of this word, equilibrium, or mental balance, the motto of my life. I saw so many of my fellow survivors of Hitler's death camps, wallowing in pity, unable to forgive, forget and enjoy life again. Physically they survived, but emotionally they bore the scars so deeply that they became living victims of the war. "I made up my mind that I would not let this happen to me," she declares. "I would live a life in equilibrium; I would remember my past and keep it alive so that future generations would not allow another Holocaust to happen anywhere in the world. But, at the same time I would live each day to the fullest and enjoy life and try to be happy." Penina has indeed found that balance in her life.

a good name is worth more than money

Abe climbed out of the chimney to the top of the roof. The day before, the Nazis had marched all the Dachau prisoners into the hills, telling them that the Americans were not far away. The Germans had taken all the Russian prisoners of war and began to shoot them, and when Abe heard the gunshots, he knew that he was next. Instinctively, he looked for a place to hide, ran inside a building and climbed up a chimney. He stayed in the chimney the entire night and listened to the gunshots below. Now, however, Abe stood on top of the roof and saw American soldiers. Of course, he was unrecognizable because he was covered in chimney soot, but that didn't matter. Abe couldn't believe it. He was free.

Abraham Podber was born in Vishneve, Poland, on September 9, 1919. He led a good life in his early years, going to school and helping his parents earn a living. Their Gentile neighbors were not always friendly, but all in all, Vishneve was a good place to be. That is, until the Germans came.The Nazis occupied Vishneve when Abe was 19 or 20 years old. At first the Jews thought that everything would be fine; they didn't know what the Germans would do or expect. However, after the Jews were confined to a ghetto, people began to realize that

maybe everything wouldn't be okay. "[The Germans] put 10 families in a house!" exclaims Abe, and conditions quickly worsened.

One Friday night, a man hurried into the house and frantically advised Abe's family to run into the woods, so Abe fled. In the forest there was nothing for Abe to eat, but at least he was alive. Others, such as Abe's father, were not that lucky. The Germans herded most of the town's Jews into the local synagogue and then brought them to the fields where they were murdered. "They killed everyone in the city," recalls Abe quietly in his thick Yiddish accent. He begins to cry as memories buried for many years surface.

After the slaughter of the Vishneve Jews, the Germans discovered Abe and transported him to a work camp. From 1942 to 1945, Abe worked in Dachau. The Nazis gathered a large group of prisoners together and asked for a locksmith. Abe had never made a lock in his life, yet he stepped forward to acknowledge that he knew how. "I risked my life," recalls Abe. "I knew my life was finished." That one small action gave Abe a chance at survival. It was perhaps a small chance, but Abe had a strong will to live.

As it turns out, the Nazis never asked Abe to make a lock. It is a good thing too. Abe feels sure that if the Germans had found out that he had lied, he would have been killed. Ironically, although he was saved to be a locksmith, Abe was put to work cleaning camp worker transport trains. "They told me 'if you don't do the job, we will kill you,'" says Abe. So Abe worked on the trains until the end of the war.

One day after operating the trains, Abe's boss gave him two loaves of bread. Abe hid them in his coat so he could take them back to friends in the camp. As he walked back to camp, a suspicious guard stopped him, and the bread fell out of his coat. The Nazis backed him toward an electrical fence. Abe coughed loudly in order to call attention to himself. The train manager heard him and yelled out, "That's my best man!" The Nazis released him, letting him return to camp. Abe survived because of that train manager. "He was nice to me – he needed me," recalls Abe. Surprisingly, in the midst of this harrowing experience, Abe did not feel afraid or anxious. Asked why he did not fear for his life, he simply responds, "I was used to that, to the dying." Abe was surrounded by death, and the chances of survival were slim, yet he never gave up hope of liberation and survival.

Crawling out of a soot-laden chimney, liberation came for Abe in May 1945. From 1945 to 1949, Abe stayed in a displaced person's camp. He worked in the kitchen peeling potatoes for the American soldiers. "I was lucky," says Abe. He had survived the war and was beginning to rebuild his life. It was during his years in the DP camp that Abe met his wife, Phyllis.

Like Abe, Phyllis Podber was also a war survivor. Phyllis Sunshine was born in Sedlech, Poland, on August 28, 1928. In 1939, when Phyllis was just 11 years old, the Germans invaded Sedlech. Her family, recognizing the danger, fled to her cousin's town, hoping eventually to cross the border to Russia. The Russians caught the Sunshine family as they attempted to cross the border, sending them, with the promise of a better life, to a work camp in Magnitogorsk, Siberia. She and her family remained in the camp, and at only 12 years old, Phyllis worked in a factory making boots and shoes. "Whatever they told me to do, I did," says Phyllis. Her father got sick during the war years and died in Siberia.

After the war, 17-year-old Phyllis left Russia and came to live in the DP camp in Ulm, Germany. She worked there knitting sweaters, shawls, and hats for those who needed them. Phyllis had been in the DP camp for three years when she met her husband, Abe. Abe's brother said to him, "You know what? We have a good-looking girl for you." Phyllis and Abe were married less than six months later.

In 1949, the Podbers gained passage to America. The Jewish Joint Distribution Committee in Europe sent them to Atlanta, and they have lived there since. Life after the war was far from easy. Both knew very little English and struggled to make a living. Abe opened a grocery store that helped him provide for his family and worked in the grocery business for the majority of his adult life. The Podbers have three children and four grandchildren. They are extremely proud that they moved to America and were able to provide for their children. Phyllis says, "[We are] not well to do, but a name sometimes is worth more than money. We have a nice family. Not everything is success in money. My kids are nice boys and everyone knows them. We've made a good life." Abe proudly chimes in, "I gave them a college education. I gave them the same thing that American children have."

The Podbers are both active members of their synagogue, Congregation Shearith Israel. "I believe in God very much," says Abe confidently. "[During the war] you didn't think about religion; you thought about staying alive." However, he believes that God should have helped people during the war. "How can you take a little child and kill him?" he asks, his face filled with emotion. "How can that be?"

Despite all their hardships and struggles, the Podbers managed to survive the war and make a life for themselves and their children in Atlanta, Georgia. The war was part of their life. There is no getting around it, no avoiding it. Yet they survived to become a proud, family-oriented, religious family.

glossary of terms

Afikomen – Greek word for dessert – the matzah eaten to conclude the Passover Seder

Bar Mitzvah – coming of age ceremony for children age 13

BETAR – right wing Zionist movement

Black Market – illegal trading of goods and money to avoid wartime controls

BRECHA – underground resistance group

Challah – braided bread eaten on Friday nights and holidays

Cheder – Hebrew School

Chumash – Five Books of Moses

Death March – forced walk near the war's end to hide evidence of Holocaust

Gabbai – usher at services who orchestrates Torah readings

Gestapo – Nazi secret police

Ghetto – a walled in part of a city in which Jews were required to live

Hasidism – East European Jewish sect of pious Jews

Hazzan – cantor

HIAS – Hebrew Immigrant Aid Society

IRGUN – freedom fighters in Palestine

Jewish Joint Distribution Committee – organization that supplies and assists survivors

Jewish National Fund – fund for building the State of Israel

Matzah – unleavened bread eaten on Passover

Minyan – group of ten people needed for prayer service

Neshama – soul

ORT – rehabilitation and job training institute

Payis(ot) – ear lock of hair

Pesach – Holiday of Passover celebration the exodus from Egypt

Pogrom – government sponsored riot against a minority

Resistance – underground organizations that plotted and fought against the Nazis

Rosh Hashana – Jewish New Year

S.S. – Hitler's own troops who led the genocide

Secure Des Enfants – French underground that saved Jewish children

Shachar – Hebrew word meaning dawn

Shavuot – spring holiday celebrating the receiving of the Torah

Siddur – prayer book

T'fillin – phylacteries wore during weekday prayer

T'naim- pre-nuptial agreement

Talmud – rabbinic writings on Jewish law

Torah – Scroll of the Five Books of Moses

UNRRA – United Nationals Relief and Rehabilitation Administration

Yeshiva – Jewish school of higher learning

Yom Kippur – Day of Atonement

ZOA – Zionist Organization of America